First They Killed My Father

EXT. PHNOM PENH APARTMENT BALCONY - DAY

April 1975

We are inside a POV. Walking towards a balcony.

We pass a TV where news about the Vietnam war coming to an end is playing. We see a reflection in the television. We see our reflection. A little girl. LOUNG. The news then shows the evacuation of the American embassy in Phnom Penh Cambodia. A Helicopter takes off from the embassy. The little girl turns and walks toward a view not dissimilar to the one near the American embassy on the news.

Little caramel colored legs and feet on a balcony. The edge of a skirt in the wind identifies the child as a little girl. She begins to climb to the top of the railing. Her little hands and feet. The sound of a helicopter coming towards her. Finally she reaches the top. She watches as a helicopter almost identical to the one on the television flies low over her head. This brave free spirited little girl is LOUNG. At five she stands looking out over city from the third floor. Her POV of her feet. Toes wiggling. The city below.

The streets are mostly empty except for a few street vendors. Some shops are closed, some shops are open, there are sand bags in front of some houses. A few people ride in Cyclos. A few on motorcycles. Not much movement.

Loung watches the people. (Their clothing and style help us to know it's 1975.)

EXT. PHNOM PHEN STREETS

Loung continues to watch.

Military police officers walk the streets.

The front of some shops sandbags covering the glass entrances making them less than welcoming.

Loung notices FOUR YOUNG MEN (peasant revolutionaries) sit along a wall staring angrily at well to do couples shopping in the market. Loung doesn't understand the look on their faces but it makes her uncomfortable.

OMITTED

A billboard for a movie poster across the street catches her eye.

                    MA (O.S.)
          Loung. Come down.

Loung looks to her mother. MA is admired in Cambodia for her
height, slender build and light skin. She is a very
beautiful, very elegant woman of Chinese decent. Ma has GEAK,
Loung's three year old sister, in her arms. Luong jumps down
and goes to her.

Cambodian News Years has just past. Red decorations still on
the wall. Happy New Years (in french) hangs on the wall.

Ma puts Geak down and the girls play or share a fruit plate
Ma has put out.

Loung watches as Geak's fruit drips all over her dress. (This
can be anything from toys to fruit. The point is for the
child to notice sweet things before the war and for the
audience to get used to a child's view of the world)

OMITTED

INT. PHNOM PENH APARTMENT - LATE DAY

PA and a COLLEAGUE of his enter the room. Loung jumps into
his arms. Pa is loved for his generous heart. He reminds
Loung of a teddy bear. His eyes are warm and brown and shaped
like the moon. Loung plays with the four stripes on his
uniform. Pa greets her and asks about her day.

Pa's Colleague seems concerned but remains professional. They
speak in french (no translation as Loung can't understand as
he intends).

          COLLEAGUE   COLLEAGUE
Les Américains nous   The Americans have abandoned
abandonnent.   us. They have all already
Ils sont déjà tous partis,   left, the ambassador and the
ambassadeur, attaché   military attache...
militaire…

            PA   PA.
C'est là notre grande erreur   It was a huge error to
d'avoir cru en eux.   believe in them.

COLLEAGUE	COLLEAGUE.
Qui aurait cru qu'ils abandonnent un peuple qui se bat pour sa liberté ? Les Khmers rouges sont déjà à Takmao et à l'ouest ils sont en passe de contrôler l'aéroport de Pochentong. Nos forces ne tiendront pas 48 heures de plus, il faudrait négocier maintenant.	Who would of guessed they would have abandoned the people fighting for freedom. The Khmer Rouge are already at Takmao and they have passed the west, controlling Pochentong airport. Our forces cannot hold for more than 48 hours, we have to negotiate now.

PA	PA.
Il ne faut pas trop s'inquiéter. Hou Youn, Hou Nim, Khieu Samphan sont des nationalistes. On trouvera bien une solution entre Cambodgiens.	Don't worry to much. Hou Youn, Hou Nim, Khieu Samphan are nationalist. We will find a good solution between us as Cambodians.

Because she can't understand, Loung looses interest and crawls out of his arms.

(They could turn on the radio at one point and it could add to the information about situation.)

INT. PHNOM PENH APARTMENT LIVING ROOM - LATE DAY

Loung walks into the living room where her brother KIM, ten, listening to music on a record player. His records and comics are spread out all over the floor. Like all older brothers he likes to give his little sisters trouble.

Loung reaches for the crickets (or colorful fruit) he is eating. He chops at her arm kung fu style. He does a huanaman (monkey king) kick. (Possibly in Pa's helmet)

CHOU helps with Geak.

Loung looks up at KHOUY and MENG her eldest brothers who have just walked in the door. Meng greets her with a smile and musses her hair. He is gentle and soft spoken like Pa. Khouy is cool with his sunglasses and long hair. (Maybe he brings something to Kim or tried out a new record.)

INT. PHNOM PENH APARTMENT - EVENING

Everyone sits at the table. Set with elegance. Ma and KEAV Loung's beautiful older sister, help serve the food. Loung watches their hands. So delicate. Their grace and poise is a mystery to her.

CLOSE UP - Loung's POV of food. Loung drops two whole peppers in her soup and Pa looks on approvingly. She crushes the peppers against the side of her bowl with a spoon.

Loung likes the smile he gives her; so she again reach her chopsticks toward the pepper dish, knocking over the salt shaker, which rolls like a fallen log onto the floor.

Ma seems upset but Pa smiles forgivingly. What Loung loves most about Pa is the way he smiles not only with his mouth but also with his eyes.

Loung always restless, kicking her feet under the table.

INT. PHNOM PHEN APARTMENT - NIGHT

Keav helps to get Loung, Chou and Geak ready for bed. Loung in her pyjamas being told to stop jumping on the bed. (details - again important to feel her life before war)

EXT. PHNOM PENH APARTMENT - DAY

{NOTE: This sequence will begin with the arrival of LON NOL (Government) troops entering the city believing that a truce has been agreed.}
At the beginning, the first to enter the city were the Lon Nol soldiers, they put the guns down and they raised white flags and people applauded because it was for them the end of the war and the end of bloody fighting in the city. Later, the Khmer Rouge soldiers entered with closed expressions on their faces. They did not talk to anyone. Most of the Khmer Rouge entered the city by walking, to secure the streets. Their chiefs were riding in jeeps but very few. Some were driving motorbikes.

It is the high heat of the afternoon. Loung plays hopscotch with Chou and their friends on the street in front of their flat.

Sounds of giggles are taken over by the thunder of engines in the distance. Everyone stops what they are doing and watches the tanks roar into the city. The Lon Nol soldiers waving white flags. Smiling. People cheer.

Then Loung sees something else coming. Trucks.

Minutes later, the mud-covered old trucks heave and bounce as they pass slowly in front of Loung. Green, gray and black, these cargo trucks sway back and forth on bald tires, spitting out dirt and engine smoke as they roll on.

In the back of the trucks, men wearing faded black long pants and long-sleeve black shirts, many with tire shoes and with red sashes cinched tightly around their waists and red scarves tied around their foreheads, stand body to body. Most look young and all are dark-skinned, like the peasant workers.

With long rifles in their arms or strapped across their backs, they look over the crowds the way the king does when he passes by. There is no cheering for them.

Loung waves at the soldiers even though she doesn't know exactly why. She sees more trucks coming.

INT. PHNOM PENH APARTMENT - DAY

Loung runs up to the apartment stairs. Her little legs run as fast as they can but the stairs feel like they go on forever.

INT. PHNOM PENH APARTMENT - DAY

Loung finds Pa on the balcony with Meng and Kim. They seem tense. She watches them.

EXT. PHNOM PHEN APARTMENT - DAY

> LON NOL MILITARY COMMANDER
> My brothers, we must avoid any effusion of blood. Put your guns down. We will negotiate with our brothers from the other side. We are all Khmer. We all love our country, our nation. We will…

A KR takes the megaphone brutally.

> KHMER ROUGE WITH MEGAPHONE
> Angkar has won throughout the country over the Khmer Republic. Lon Nol are traitors. Angkar need not negotiate with anyone or any group. The traitors must accept defeat. Give up your guns. There will be no negotiation

The Clique of Lon Nol soldiers form a group.

> KHMER ROUGE WITH MEGAPHONE (CONT'D)
> America will bomb the city. You must leave now! Take as little as you can. No one can stay here.
> (MORE)

                         KHMER ROUGE WITH MEGAPHONE (CONT'D)
            The United States will bomb the
            city! Leave and stay in the
            countryside for three days!

Loung doesn't understand.

Loung stares at a man holding a megaphone standing on a jeep.

A KR soldier fires shots to open a door and clear out a
building. Loung claps her hands over her ears and hides her
face against Keav's chest. People push and shove one another
in a frenzy.

Ma now standing behind Loung has heard.

                    MA
            Loung quickly, go eat your lunch.

OMITTED

INT. PHNOM PENH KITCHEN - DAY

Loung goes into the kitchen. Her lunch is waiting for her.
Everyone else has already eaten. She sits and eats.

After a few minutes, Ma rushes into the kitchen with Keav and
begins to toss aluminum bowls, plates, spoons, forks, and
knives into a big pot. The silverware clangs noisily, making
Loung jittery. Then picking up a cloth bag, she throws bags
of sugar, salt, dried fish, uncooked rice, and canned foods
into it.

                    MA
            We will be leaving for a few days.
            Gather your things.

                    LOUNG
            But Ma?

                    MA
            Gather your things.

Loung shovels down a few more bites and gets up.

INT. PHNOM PHEN APARTMENT - DAY

Loung follows Ma into the bedroom where she sees her and Keav
sewing jewelry into a jacket lining.

She then moves from the bedroom to the living room, taking pictures of her family and the Buddha off the walls and piling them into her arms.

In the bathroom, Kim throws soap, shampoo, towels, and other assorted items into a pillowcase.

>   MA
>   (to Loung)
>   Are you finished yet?

Loung nods "no".

>   MA (CONT'D)
>   Hurry and change your shirt. The
>   one you're wearing is dirty.

INT. PHNOM PENH APARTMENT LOUNG'S ROOM - DAY

Loung pokes her head into her bedroom and spies Chou shoving clothes into a bag. On the bed, Geak sits quietly playing with a handheld mirror while Chou throws our brushes, combs, and hairpins into her school bag.

Loung goes through her clothes and picks a yellow shirt. Chou is packing her red dress. Loung remembers to pack her matching one.

OMITTED

EXT. PHNOM PENH STREETS - DAY

The family head out of the apartment. The chaos of the city. People push and shove one another to evacuate the city. Everywhere, people are on the move. Little children cry. Women and men carry their belongings in cloth bags on their backs and their heads. They walk with short, brisk steps, demanding their children stay together, to hold each other's hands, to not get left behind.

A lone radio has been abandoned in the chaos. Loung listens to the song as she passes.

Loung moves to the Mazda parked outside but she is pulled away from it and towards the old family truck in the back. The family pile into the truck. The old pickup truck creaks and squeaks as Khouy throws a cloth bag and water can onto its floor. In front, Pa ties a large white cloth to the antenna while Meng ties another piece to the side mirrors.

I/E. TRUCK - DAY

The traffic is moving very slowly.

Loung looks out. Their truck inches on in the streets,
allowing them a safe view of the scene.

EXT. PHNOM PENH STREETS - DAY

Families on the move. Chaos. The KR soldiers are everywhere.
There are so many of them around, giving orders into their
bullhorns cradling rifles in their arms.

Loung notices the other children. The fear on their faces.

Small mountains of guns fill the sidewalk as government
soldiers turn over their weapons to the men in black. The
soldiers are then put into a truck and driven off.

Loung buries her face into Keav's chest, her arms tight
around her waist. Chou sits silently on the other side of
Keav, her eyes shut. Beside them, Khouy and Meng sit stone-
faced, watching the exodus.

(FACT- TWO MILLION PEOPLE EVACUATED THE CITY WITHIN 72 HOURS)

I/E. TRUCK - DAY

Later - Loung burrows under her scarf to hide from the sun.
Her eye lids struggle to stay open. Her POV of her hair
whiping about her face. The sun shining on it. Keav wraps the
end of Loungs scarf over her mouth an nostrils to keep the
dust out.

> KEAV
> Don't look over the truck. Keep
> your head down.

Loung pretends to follow her sisters orders but peeks over
the edge.

Loung sees a doctor assisting a pregnant woman out of the
hospital. A KR soldier telling the doctor to evacuate people
more quickly. The doctor begs him. He moves him aside and
guides staff and patients out with his rifle. She sees a
hospital evacuated. Some people being pushed in carts or
hospital beds by their relatives.

Soldiers in black knocking on doors with their gun buts and
evacuating people from their homes.

OMITTED

EXT. PHNOM PENH - DAY

High wide shot of the chaos of the city. The truck slowly
makes it's way through the crowded streets.

I/E. TRUCK - DAY

As they move further from the city, the high rise apartments
disappear and thatched-roofed huts take their place. The
paved boulevard gives way to dusty roads. Tall elephant grass
and prickly brown bushes have replaced the tall trees.

As far as Loung can see, there are people marching in the
roads while huts stand empty and rice field are left
unattended. (See some areas affected by bombing - possibly
one or two plate shots)

EXT. ROADSIDE - MAGIC HOUR

The sun is setting. The masses silhouetted as they continue
along the road.

EXT. ROADSIDE - NIGHT

Hours later - the truck pulls over.

The fields are lit up with small fires illuminating the faces
of the women squatting near them, preparing meals. Loung
looks around. In the darkness she can still make out
thousands of people milling around, or walking to unknown
destinations. Others, like them have stopped to rest for the
night along the roadside.

Later -

Ma and Keav prepare the meal from the food Ma had packed.
Chou is brushing Geak's hair, being careful not to pull it.
They squat in the darkness eating their food. (discuss Ma
trading jewels for items or food)

OMITTED

EXT. ROADSIDE - NIGHT

Loung is tucked in by Ma in the back of the truck. While Ma Loung, Chou and Geak sleep in the bed of the truck, the older kids sleep on the ground with Pa. It's a warm breezy night, the kind that requires no blankets.

Loung can't sleep. She looks up at the vastness of the sky. The dark sky is full of shining bright stars. Some blink at her. She winks back and closes her eyes.

EXT. ROADSIDE - MORNING

Loung opens her eyes to find her family is already packing up. They look tired with their hair sticking out in all directions.

Someone is yelling. Loung looks around. A group of Khmer Rouge soldiers are yelling at everyone to keep moving. Loung stares at their guns.

Meng helps her up and gives her comfort.

The KR soldier signals for Pa to move away from the truck. Pa steps out.

> ROAD BLOCK KR
> You comrade! The Angkar needs your truck. You no longer will need it.

Loung looks to Pa for his response. He simply lowers his eyes and nods.

> PA
> (softly to his family)
> Everyone grab what you can carry.

Loung watches as her siblings begin to pack.

> KHMER ROUGE SOLDIER ROADSIDE
> Comrade! Angkar needs your watch!

> PA
> Certainly.

Loung watches as Pa's shoulders bend forward in submission. He takes the watch off his wrist. Pa does not look the soldier in the eyes as he hands over the watch.

Loung watches as a YOUNG KR walks up to Meng and Khouy. He smiles at them. A strange smile as he takes their watches. He gives Keav a look.

The soldiers look at Pa's watch with suspicion.

                         KHMER ROUGE SOLDIER ROADSIDE
          This is very nice. Who are you to
          have such a nice watch?

                         PA
          It was a gift from my boss.

 KHMER ROUGE SOLDIER ROADSIDE   KHMER ROUGE SOLDIER ROADSIDE.
Tu travailles pour le   You work for the government?
gouvernment?

He walks towards Pa with the barrel of the gun pointing at
his mid section. Loung stares at the gun. It is right at her
eye level. She can hardly breathe. He speaks the phrase
again and watches Pa's reaction.

After a very tense moment, Pa seems to pass the test and the
family is suddenly moved on.

As they walk on Loung notices some men with long hair who
seem to have been selected and are being held. Ma also
notices.

OMITTED

Content from Scene 42 and 43 merged into Scene 45.

Content from Scene 44 merged into Scene 41.

EXT. ROAD - DAY

The sun is hot on Loung's back. It burns through her black hair. She looks at Chou and sees beads of sweat collect along her hair line and upper lip.

Everywhere they go people are walking in all directions carrying their belongings. Soldiers with guns move them along.

They walk from the break of day until the dark of the evening. Loung Looks at her fingers and holds up one finger then two.

EXT. ROADSIDE - EVENING

Ma and Pa guides the children to an area roadside where they sit in silence and eat the dried fish they had packed. Ma has a small pot of sugar (OR BUYS IT FROM A FAMILY) They all have a taste of it. Loung rolls it in her fingers and licks every last bit.

Later - Ma is cutting off Khouy's long hair.

Loung sees her father walking off on his own. She follows him with her eyes. He finds a secret place in the shade, behind a tree, and goes to his knees.

Loung moves closer. She sees he is digging a hole. A moment later he pulls his ID cards and his work ties and buries them.

She doesn't understand and moves quickly back so he doesn't see her.

Gone is the air of mystery and excitement; now Luong is simply afraid.

OMITTED

EXT. ROAD - MORNING

Along the road, the bombed buildings, the scars of war.

It's the third day on the road. Loung walks with a little more bounce in her step. She looks at her fingers and holds up two then three. She makes her way up to Pa.

> LOUNG
> Pa, the soldiers said we can return home after three days.

Loung tugs at Pa's trousers.

> PA
> No, Loung.

> LOUNG
> But it's the third day.

> PA
> (sadly)
> We have to keep walking.

> LOUNG
> Pa, I'm hungry and my feet hurt.

Loung stops walking. She stands still on the road and lets go of the rice pot to wipe the dirt and tears from her cheeks.

> LOUNG (CONT'D)
> Let's go home. I just want to go home.

The red dust from the road and the sweat on her little body have mixed to create a layer of mud on her skin, making it dry and itchy.

Pa walks over to Keav and takes a ball of sticky rice out of the pot she is carrying. He walks back to Loung and hands her the food. Her eyes look down at the ground in shame but she takes the food anyway. Silently, he strokes her hair while she eats the rice between the chocking sobs.

Pa bends down and looks Loung in the eyes.

> PA
> We cannot go home tonight.

> LOUNG
> But they said three days.

> PA
> We have to keep walking.

Reluctantly, Loung does what Pa tells her. Everybody has to carry something, so she pick the smallest item in the pile, the rice pot.

As she walks, the pot becomes heavier and heavier in her hands as the sun climbs higher and higher in the sky. The metal handle digs and burns the palms of her hands. Sometimes she carries it with two hands in front of her, other times she switches the pot from her right to her left arm, but it seems no matter how she carries it the pot painfully bangs into some part of her leg.

Later- Loung is losing hope that they can go home tonight. Tired and hungry, she drags her feet, taking smaller and smaller steps until she is far behind everyone else.

Pa gently walks over and cleans her face with his hand. He then takes the rice pot and carries it for her.

With Geak on her hip, Ma walks over to Loung and wraps a scarf around her head to protect her from the sun. As she walks on Loung watches Geak in her arms. He feet dangling off Ma's hip. Loung wishes she was a baby and could be carried.

She sees many people around her that are worse off than herself.

Hours later-

As the hot sun beats down on them, the family continues to walk.
- for the landscape : On the road from Phnom Penh to Kam Baul, there is very little forest.

- KR soldiers do not have their arms across their back. They have AK47 that they carry on the side or in front of them. (See photos archives).
- most of the time, the KR cadres, the kamapibal, who manage evacuation, have no arms. Or maybe just a handgun.
- along the road of evacuation, there are KR patrols

Loung watches as a woman breast feeds her baby wrapped to her chest as she walks.

Loung sees a KR soldier. She quickly turns her face away and walks to catch up with Pa.

Loung studies the face of the father then quickly turns her face away and walks to catch up with Pa.

EXT. CHECKPOINT - DAY

By noontime they have reached the Khmer Rouge's military check-point. The checkpoint consists of no more than a few small makeshift tents with trucks parked beside them. There are many soldiers at this base, and it is easy to recognize them because they wear identical loose-fitting black pajama pants and shirts. Even the female KR have very distinct hair cuts. All carry identical guns slung across their backs. They move quickly from place to place with fingers on the triggers of their weapons, pacing back and forth in front of the crowd, giving instructions into a bullhorn.

> KAMAPIBAL
> You are not allowed to pass until
> we have cleared you. Stand with
> your family in a line.

The Commander continues.

> KAMAPIBAL (CONT'D)
> Anyone who has worked as a public
> servant, official, police, or
> military, step up to the right
> table to register for work.

Loung glances at Pa then looks quickly away. She feels sick. Pa gathers their family and stands them in a line with the other peasant farmers.

> PA
> (whispering)
> Remember, we are workers. Give
> these men whatever they want and
> don't argue.

In front of them, the line splits in two as a large group of ex-soldiers, government workers, and former politicians walk over to the table to register for work. Loung's heart pounds quickly against her chest, but she says nothing and leans against Pa's legs. He reaches down and puts his hand on top of her head. It stays there as if protecting her from the sun and the soldiers. After a few minutes, her head feels cooler and her heartbeat slows. (Artists with long hair and possibly a guitar are taken away)

A KR soldier opens a bag of another family discovering a bundle of money.

>   KR CHECKPOINT SOLDIER
>   You do not need this. (Holding the
>   money) There are no longer any
>   rich, there are no longer any poor.
>   Let us all live in equality!

Ahead of them in the line, Khmer Rouge soldiers tells something to the crowd, but Loung cannot understand all of what they say.

>   KR CHECKPOINT SOLDIER (CONT'D)
>   When the Angkar questions you,
>   answer loyally.

Then one Khmer Rouge soldier roughly jerks a bag off of one man's shoulder and dumps its contents on the ground. From this pile, a Khmer Rouge soldier picks up an old Lon Nol army uniform. The Khmer Rouge soldier sneers at the man and pushes him to another Khmer Rouge soldier standing beside him. The soldier then moves on to the next family. Eyes downcast, shoulders slumped, arms hanging loosely on both sides of him, the man with the Lon Nol uniform in his bag does not fight as another Khmer Rouge soldier points and pushes him away with the butt of his rifle.

Loung feels the heat of the sun move down her back. We notice the shadows moving. Hours have gone by.

A Khmer Rouge soldier approaches them, Loung leans closer to Pa and reaches up for his hand. Pa's hand is much too big for hers, so She is only able to wrap her fingers around his index finger.

>   KOM BAUL SOLDIER
>   What do you do?

>   PA
>   I work as a packer in the shipping
>   port.

>   KOM BAUL SOLDIER
>   (to Ma)
>   And you, what do you do?

Loung notices Ma's eyes focus on the ground and she shifts, Geak's weight on her hips.

>   MA
>   I sell old clothes in the market.

The soldier rummages through all their bags one by one.

He takes money and Kim's comic books. (Discuss what else would be taken)

He takes the red dresses Loung and Chou had packed.

Loung follows the dress with her eyes, focusing all her energy on it, wanting desperately to rescue it.

Her first red dress, the one Ma made for her for the New Year's celebration.

MEMORY--

INT. PHNOM PENH APARTMENT

Flashes of color - Loung remembers Ma taking her measurements, holding the soft chiffon cloth against her body, and asking her if she liked it. Ma smiles at Loung pleased with how pretty the color looks on her. Loung sees herself in the mirror.

MEMORY ENDS

Then he bends down and lifts the lid of the rice pot next to Pa's feet. Gripping Pa's finger even tighter, Loung's heart races as the soldier checks the pot. His face is close to hers; she concentrates on her dirty toes. She dare not look into his eyes.

She peaks. She looks right at him.

>   KOM BAUL SOLDIER
>   All right, you are cleared. You may
>   go.

>   PA
>   (meekly)
>   Thank you comrade.

The soldier is already looking past Pa and merely waves his hand for them to hurry on.

EXT. ROAD - DAY

Passing the checkpoint safely, they walk on. A few miles down the road the sound of gunshots ring out in the distance behind Loung. She watches as a flock of black birds explode into the sky.

EXT. ROAD - LATE DAY

Later - As she walks, Loung watches as the sun goes to sleep behind the mountains and the world becomes a place of shadows and shapes once again. Sees a body in the field. He wears a uniform like Pa's.

EXT. ROADSIDE - DUSK (ADJUST DEPENDING LOTUS FLOWERS)

In the mass of people, Pa finds them a spot of unoccupied grass near the side of the road.

Loung and Chou walk around and find a pond full of lotus flowers. Kim finds a small area full of fish. The children, as children do, explore the area.

Later - Ma puts Geak down next to Loung and tells her to keep an eye on her. Sitting next to her, Loung is struck by how Geak looks. Breathing quietly, she fights to keep her eyelids open, but in the end she loses and falls to sleep. Loung puts her arm around her sister in a protective way. She lies down on a small bundle of clothes. Quickly, Loung also falls asleep.

LOUNG DREAMS

EXT. STREET

In her dream, fireworks crackle and boom noisily, she rejoices in the New Year celebration. Everything is red. Chinese firecrackers explode. Smoke rises. Confetti paper falls onto Loung's face as she runs through the bits of paper and white smoke.

LOUNG'S DREAM ENDS

EXT. ROADSIDE - MORNING

Fireworks from the dream turn into gunshots in the distance. Loung wakes up the next morning to the voices of her brothers and father whispering to each other about what went on in the night. She can't hear but they look concerned.

Keav takes her hand, grabs her things and leads her on.

EXT. ROAD - MORNING

Loung's POV - Pa carrying Geak and reassuring Kim.

People see along the road the scars of war.

Loung feels Keav's hand pull at her, and her feet automatically move in her sisters direction. With Loung's hand in hers, they catch up with the rest of the family and continue their fourth day of marching.

EXT. ROAD - DAY

On their walk, the soldiers are everywhere, prodding them along. They point and give directions with their guns.

In the scorching April heat, Loung watches as many older people become ill from heatstroke and dehydration, although they dare not rest. When someone falls ill, the family throws out his belongings, puts the sick person on someone's back and march on.

Loung notices a few lifeless bodies laid in a row on the side of the road. She focuses on their feet.

The road ahead of them shimmers in the heat, and the dust swells are everywhere, burning Loung's eyes.

In the distance, her eyes focus on a lone man with a wagon pulled by two yellow skinny cows. It is strange that he is traveling against the flow of traffic. All of a sudden, she is startled by Ma's scream. Between loud, halting sobs Ma manages to say-

                    MA
          It's you Uncle Leang!

With their hands in the air and bodies jumping up and down, they wave excitedly to their uncle. UNCLE LEANG waves one hand back and moves his ox cart in their direction. He comes to a stop a few feet from them, and all at once they rush toward him. He takes Ma into his arms with Pa standing quietly beside them.

Uncle Leang hands Ma a package from the cart, she opens the package of food, sweet rice, fish and bamboo sticks.

                    UNCLE LEANG
          I've been looking for you since I
          heard.

Standing next to Uncle Leang, Loung has to tilt her head back as far as she can to see his face because he is so tall. All she can see is the shape of his thin lips and wide, black nostrils that flare once every few seconds as he talks to Ma. At almost six feet tall, second Uncle Kim Leang hovers above all of them.

OMITTED

EXT. ROADSIDE - DAY

While Pa and Ma talk to Loung's uncle, Loung quickly claims a seat in the wagon with Chou and Geak. She stares at the skinny cows. She wonders if they are strong enough to be able to pull the family.
Only young children can be on the wagon with the uncle.

EXT. ROAD / OX CART - DAY TO DUSK

As the sun begins to set. Their trail takes them on a gravel road along Route 26 westward. No matter where they go or in which direction they turn, there are people marching ahead and behind them. In the midst of the crowd,

Their wagon passes a Khmer Rouge village without stopping. Houses on stilts and men in black with checkered scarfs. Some of their children are in the bright green fields catching fish with rods.

Further down the road Loung sees a pagoda with KR soldiers holding men prisoner. Beyond them in the distance she sees soldiers watching as Monks are made to tend the fields. Loung looks at the faces of the Monks. They are put to work as if they are being punished. She feels sad for them.

The cattle wagon keeps moving.

They veer westward, leaving their roadside companions far behind.

Later-

Somewhere between Bat Deng and Krang Truop, Loung falls asleep.

HER POV GOES OUT OF FOCUS.

EXT. KRANG TRUOP - EARLY MORNING

Loung slowly opens her eyes. Five days after leaving their home in Phnom Penh, the family arrives at Krang Truop. A small dusty village surrounded by rice fields as far as the eye can see.

INT. UNCLE LEANG'S HUT - MORNING

Loung enters Uncle Leang's hut. Uncle Leang and his wife have six children, so with the nine new people it makes seventeen under one roof. There are objects that show Uncle Leang had been a middle class farmer before the Khmer Rouge took over.

Loung climbs into Pa's arms.

>   LOUNG
>   The village is so poor.

>   PA
>   (strong)
>   So are we. And from now on if
>   anyone asks, we say we are workers.
>   We can not go back to the city. You
>   must stop thinking we can go back.

Pa has never spoken to her this way. It finally sinks in. She trembles with fear. He holds her in his arms as her eyes water and her lips tremble.

EXT./INT. UNCLE LEANG'S HUT - DAY

Loung's POV of the rice fields. She removes her clothes and hands them to Chou who is already washed and in a sarong.

Loung washes herself outside. There is a big round container that looks like a three-foot-tall clay flowerpot. Then she reaches into the container and takes a bowl full of water and pours it over herself.

She becomes shy when she sees her little cousins watching her.

EXT. UNCLE LEANG'S HUT - DAY

The family clothes hang to dry. Pa helps Uncle repair a fish trap. He is clumsy because he does not know how to do it properly. They share a hot tea and smoke tobacco. A NEIGHBOR is with them.

                    NEIGHBOR
Is it true everyone has evacuated
Phnom Phen? (Pa nods) Did the
Americans bomb the city?

                    PA
Angkar asked us to leave. I heard
no bombings.

                    UNCLE LEANG
Here, in the village, Americans
have bombed for many years.
Sometimes three days in a row. We
had to harvest during the night.

He pauses deep in thought.

> NEIGHBOR
> They destroyed my house. My cows. I
> now support the Khmer Rouge
> revolution. We want a new society,
> without poor people, without rich
> people. We don't need the
> capitalists. The land is ours. We
> are masters of earth and water.

Nobody answers.

> UNCLE LEANG
> If you stay here you must refer to
> the village chief. You are from the
> city. You must be careful. Angkar
> knows everything.

EXT. UNCLE LEANG'S HUT - DAY

Loung wanders away towards a group of kids having a beetle
fight. Geak is loving it. Chou is not so sure.

Kim and Meng and Khouy play around doing handstands, and
teaching their cousins.

Ma and Keave are with the other women.

INT. UNCLE LEANG'S HUT - NIGHT

Lying on wooden planks Loung watches Chou tossing and
turning. Ma sits on a mat nearby holding Geak, who sleeps
quietly in her arms. She looks around the room at her
sleeping family. Loung overhears a discussion underneath the
floorboards. She looks through the slats.

> AUNT KEANG
> We cannot keep them with us. We
> will be killed.

> UNCLE LEANG
> She is my sister.

> AUNT KEANG
> You know there is no consideration
> for family.

They continue whispering but Loung can't make out what they
are saying. She looks over at Ma, wondering if she has
heard.

EXT. UNCLE LEANG'S HUT - EARLY MORNING

Loung watching Uncle Leang. Wondering if he will say
anything. Life on the farm starts before the sun rises. The
clothes are now dry on the line.

Washing up. Breakfast. (Scraps to pigs? Feed for chickens?)

EXT. KRANG TRUOP - MORNING

Loung walks into the fields.

Using the traps made last night, they catch fish.

The buffalo's are brought in to graze.

Loung looks around she cannot shake the feeling someone is
watching her. She looks around anxious.

OMITTED

Content from Scene 89 has been merged into Scene 77AA.

OMITTED

Later-

Loung watching her cousins and neighbors play.

Loung walks past Pa who sits quietly outside by himself. She enters the hut but turns when she hears a cow bell. They both watch as the Village Chief approaches Uncle Leang. They both know what this means.

OMITTED

INT./EXT. UNCLE LEANG'S HUT - EVENING

Loung watches everyone around her packing. Uncle Leang, his wife, AUNT KEANG, and all the cousins are up. Beside Loung, Chou rolls up her thin blanket, folds her clothes and puts them in her pillow case. Outside, Lee Cheun scoops ladles full of cooked rice and puts it in banana leaves. Keav pokes the crackling fire to cook the dried fish while Kim fills up the petrol container with water.

Ma puts her hand to her mouth to signal to Loung to stay quiet. Loung pulls the cover over her and looks at her still blistered feet. She doesn't want to walk anymore. She wants to stay.

Pa pulls back the covers and gently pulls her from her bed. Biting back her tears she puts on her flip flops and walks toward Keav's extended hand.

Pa and Ma turn to Uncle Leang and thank him for letting them stay with him. Uncle Leang looks at her, face hanging, eyes blinking rapidly, and blesses Ma for a safe journey.

The cousins stand outside the hut to see the family off. Their hands dangle lifelessly by their sides as they watch Pa lead his family away.

EXT. REST STOP - NIGHT

By the time the family arrives at the rendezvous area on the roadside, about thirty people have already gathered there. They squat and sit on the gravel road in four family groups. Many have almond-shaped eyes, thin noses, and light skin, which suggests they might also be of Chinese descent. Their fellow travelers do not acknowledge their presence, instead they stare passively at the road. Like the family, they carry with them light bundles of clothes and small packages of food.

Loung and family sit on the gravel road next to them but no words are exchanged. In the dark of night they all wait for the truck.

Later- Loung lays in Pa's arms. The world around them remains tranquil and asleep; all that can be heard is the chirping of crickets. The moments feel like forever. Then suddenly the glaring headlights of the military truck appear and it stops before them. Pa transfers Loung from his warm arms onto the hard, cold bed of the truck. She does not want to let go of him. She does not want to leave the safety of his arms. Trucks had tarpaulins that way nobody could see people inside and people inside could not watch the road.

EXT. MILITARY TRUCK #1 - NIGHT

The ride is bumpy and loud, but the cool dawn air keeps them reasonably comfortable. Ma stares off into the distance while Geak sleeps in her arms. Loung's other siblings are half dozing, half awake while she finds safety in Pa's arms again. Everyone is very quiet as the truck drives on.

All night the truck heads northwest.

EXT. MILITARY TRUCK #1 - DAWN

The truck driver does not have Pa's driving skills, nor does he care whether those in the back bounce and bump into one another. The truck drives all day the children take small bites from the food they packed as they drive on.

OMITTED

EXT. MILITARY TRUCK #1 - EARLY MORNING

Loung wakes up in Pa's lap in the morning to see that they have arrived at a "truck stop." There are people lined up. Some just waiting. Others getting onto ox carts. Many are still asleep on the side of the road or in the grass. Sitting in the back of the truck, they dare not move until the soldiers instruct them to.

EXT. PURSAT PROVINCE - EARLY MORNING

As soon as they are told, everyone jumps off. Pa lifts Loung out of the truck and puts her on the ground next to Chou.

Loung overhears Meng and Pa talking.

> MENG
> We're not in Battambang?

> PA
> (fatigued)
> We will go where ever they choose
> to take us.

Loung looks around. She doesn't want to stay here.

OMITTED

EXT. PURSAT PROVENCE - EARLY MORNING

Ma secretly cuts open Kim's jacket, pulls out her jewelry and
hands it over to the KR.

As Pa lifts her onto the ox cart., She notices two very thin middle-aged men in loose-fitting black pajama pants and shirts standing next to them. While one writes something on small brown pads of paper with his black pen, the other points at their heads and counts as they climb onto the truck. Loung finds herself a seat where she can watch the countryside. Quickly, another family clambers onto the cart. Once all the families are on board, the two men take their notes and count again. After they are finished, the ox carts pull away.

EXT. OX CART - MORNING

The ox cart rolls away from the waiting area and onto a bumpy narrow road.

The families are quiet and somber, the only sounds come from the branches brushing against the side of the truck and the slush of mud sticking to the tires. Loung notices DAVI a beautiful teen young woman who sits with her LITTLE SISTER. DAVI'S FATHER, DAVI'S MOTHER, and DAVI'S BROTHERS are also in (or walking beside) the cart.

She looks at the ripped open part of her jacket or her mothers depending on where we choose to hide the jewels.

Loung rests her head on Pa's chest and think how lucky she is to have such a father. She looks up at Pa who seems so serious and sad. She worries for him. She misses his smile.

INT. OX CART - DAY

The Ox Cart passes a Buddhist temple that has been destroyed and is now crawling with soldiers. Pa bows his head in a moment of silence. Another man in the truck notices and looks at Pa with suspicion.

Loung looks at the temple.

LOUNG'S MEMORY--

EXT. TEMPLE (ANGKOR WAT)- DAY

Loung remembers clutching tightly to Pa's finger as they walked along wide crumbling corridors. The temple walls are decorated with magnificent detailed carvings of people, cows, wagons, daily life, and battle scenes from long ago.

Guarding the ancient steps are giant granite lions, tigers, eight-headed snakes, and elephants. Next to them, sandstone gods with eight hands who sit cross-legged on lotus flowers watch over the temple ponds. On the walls beneath the jungle vines, thousands of beautiful Apsara goddesses with big round breasts wearing only short wraparound skirts smile at visitors.

Pa leads Loung through the temple.

> LOUNG O.S.
> Meng said you were once a monk.

> PA
> (smiling)
> I was. But I met a beautiful woman
> in a pretty blue silk shirt, who's
> smile melted my heart. The same
> smile her daughters now have.

Loung smiles.

> LOUNG O.S.
> Did you live here?

> PA
> This is where the Gods live. If you
> call out, they will answer.

> LOUNG O.S.
> (yells)
> Chump leap sursdei dthai pda!
> (Hello Gods)

> ECHO
> Dthai pda! Dthai pda!

Loung grabs Pa's leg when she hears the Gods answer. Pa smiles down at her laughing.

MEMORY FADES

EXT. OX CART - DAY

Geak cries. Ma moves to her to comfort her. She holds her tightly to her breasts as if to never let her go. Loung looks at Ma's blue silk shirt and realizes why she chose to bring it with her.

EXT. RO LEAP MEETING AREA - DAY

The cart stops.

The driver orders the new arrivals to get out and wait for instructions from the village chief. Loung's family quickly jumps off the cart, leaving her behind. Standing at the edge, she fights the impulse to run and hide in the far corner.

All around the ox carts, villagers have gathered to take their first look at the new people. These villagers are all dressed in the familiar loose-fitting black pajama pants and shirts with a red-and-white checkered scarf wrapped across their shoulders or around their head. They look like an older version of the Khmer Rouge soldiers that stormed into their city, except they do not carry guns.

> SOMEONE IN THE CROWD
> Capitalists should be shot and
> killed.

> A BASE WOMAN
> Parasites!

The Base Woman walks over and spits at Pa's feet. Pa's shoulders droop low as he holds his palms together in a gesture of greeting. Loung cowers at the edge of the Ox Cart, afraid to get off. To her, the villagers look very mean, like hungry tigers ready to pounce. Their black eyes stare at her, full of contempt.

> PA
> (gently to Loung)
> Come, you have to get off the cart.

She drags her body cautiously toward him. She takes hold of Chou's hand and together they follow Ma. (While he speaks, Loung focuses on other things.)

EXT. RO LEAP MEETING AREA - CONTINUOUS

Loung looks around.

There were no soldiers in the villages, but there were chlops, it means militiamen who spy, who are security guards, who arrest...

                    RO LEAP KHMER ROUGE
              (with a heavy accent of
                people from the jungle
                area)
          Angkar never uses any object from
          imperialist and feudal society.
          All of these things create a deep
          divide between rich and poor.
          You must absolutely give up all
          personal property. Destroy
          individualism; build the collective
          spirit! Absolutely everything
          belongs to the Angkar!

Loung nestles closer to Chou and leans her head on her
shoulder. The RO LEAP VILLAGE CHIEF makes his appearance to
the crowd of new people.

OMITTED

EXT. RO LEAP MEETING AREA - DAY

                    RO LEAP KHMER ROUGE
          By wearing the same thing we rid
          ourselves of the corrupt Western
          creation of vanity. We are all
          equal. You will take these stain
          (he holds up a bowl of berries -
          makhleur in Khmer) and then mix in
          mud to dye your remaining clothes,
          removing all color.
          Renounce family ties, and adopt the
          immense family; have a
          revolutionary consciousness!

                    ALL
          Yes, comrade.

RO LEAP KHMER ROUGE
Father is now "Pok". Not Daddy or
Pa...Mother is "Meh". The Angkar
tenderly looks after you all, The
Angkar is your family now.

Loung grabs her Pa's fingers even tighter.

EXT. RO LEAP HUT - DAY

Establish the Ro Leap Village.

The family is shown to their assigned plot.

Ma sorts through the clothes. Ma and the girls work to stain
them black. First they smash the berries and stain them.
Loung watches as the clothes lose their color.

During this process the Men are coming back with planks of
wood for the house and working on the structure.

Later - the clothes in black mud are hung out to dry. Ma
sees other mothers cutting their children's hair to match the
KR. She begins with Geak. Loung watches.

OMITTED - CONTENT MERGED INTO SCENE 115

EXT. RO LEAP - LATE DAY

The bell rings, signaling mealtime. Gripping her wooden bowl
and spoon, Loung, Chou (with new haircuts) and Kim walk to
the communal kitchen while the others wait their turn. They
are separated into groups. (This is how they will now work
and eat. Girls 6-12 then older girls and women. Boys 6-12
then older boys and men.)

EXT. RO LEAP DINING AREA - BEFORE DARK

The kitchen is nothing but a long table, with no chairs or
benches, and under a thatched roof with no walls, and a few
brick ovens. On the long table sit two pots, one full of rice
and one full of soup with bits of fish inside.

There are six or seven base women stirring and scooping food
from the pots. A long line of new people has already formed
around the table. Like Loung's family, they have all changed
from their city clothing into their black pajama pants and
shirts, the only clothes they will wear from now on.

Loung looks at the long line in front of her. She stares at the many black pots filled with steamy food on the ground. The line moves quickly and silently. Under her breath she counts the heads before her, eliminating them one by one, anxiously waiting for her turn.

Loung raises her bowl to her eye level to make it easier for the comrade to serve her. She does not dare look up at the woman. Eyes focused on her bowl, Loung sees the hand dump some rice in her bowl and drop a whole small fish on top of it.

                    LOUNG
          Thank you.

EXT. DINING AREA - EARLY EVENING

Loung and her sister eat their food together. They lick the bowls clean. She looks at Davi's sister and the other new girls.

She hears an announcement and sees the next groups line up. She watches her older brothers and sisters with Ma and Pa stand in line.

Their time is up. Loung and Chou walk back towards their hut.

OMITTED

EXT. RO LEAP HUT - MORNING

Ma Keav and Loung trade items with the Base women. Loung and her sisters help sew palm tree walls for the hut. They have never done this before and are watching a family to learn. The men continue to work on the hut.

EXT. RO LEAP - EARLY MORNING

The guards patrol. Pa and the boys are working on the house.
Davi's Father and brothers are working next door to build
theirs.

OMITTED

EXT. RO LEAP - MORNING

Over the megaphone we hear the mornings announcements and
call to work. We see the rice fields begin to fill with rows
of workers.

EXT. RO LEAP - MORNING

Loung and Chou are in line with the other girls marching to
work. They pass Ma and Keav in the fields.

EXT. RO LEAP GARDEN - MORNING

Loung and Chou's first day at work. They tend to the soil to
prepare a garden. Loung looks out and sees Ma and Keav in the
rice field. Kim is in a nearby garden with the other boys.
Chlop patrol.

Later - Loung's back is hurting. She is not used to this kind   **119**
of labour. The Base Woman who spit at Pa upon arrival, walks
over. She looks at the girls and tells them they are lazy
and need to work harder.

The young girls try to hold back tears.

INT. RO LEAP HUT - DUSK

Pa finishing the roof. Loung's eyes grow heavy. She falls
asleep.

EXT. RO LEAP GARDEN - MORNING - PLANTING

We pan across a large area where we see hundreds working the
fields.

Loung and Chou work in the garden. They sweat under the hot sun.

OMITTED

EXT. RO LEAP - DAY

Loung walks back to her hut and passes her parents and older siblings working in the rice fields.

EXT. RO LEAP HUT - NIGHT

That night, Loung sneaks out of the hut past the KR on patrol and follows Pa into a meeting at the town square.

EXT. TOWN SQUARE - NIGHT

Loung and some other children are tucked away off to the side of the meeting. She watches as Ma and Pa join the others for the town meeting. Pa looks tired.

There are a couple men and women the KR have put aside. Loung wonders why and what they have done.

> RO LEAP KHMER ROUGE
> Every work site is a fiery
> battlefield. Let us be master of
> the water, master of nature. Work
> in the rice field without
> considering the skies, to grow
> three tons a hectare. If you have a
> revolutionary position, you can do
> anything Comrade. Cheyo
> revolutionary Angkar!

Fists in the air. "Cheyo! Cheyp!" The Base Girl is standing next to the KR. She points at a man and says he should confess.

The man VICTIM/INFORMANT (birthmark on his face)confesses for taking something small for his child who is sick.

He is punished and tied to a tree near the children.

OMITTED

EXT. RO LEAP

Loung and Chou on their way to work. They pass the man still
tied to the tree. Loung looks at the KR near him. Wondering
how one man could do that to another.

EXT. RO LEAP GARDEN - EARLY MORNING

Weeks have passed. (Transition possibly by coming down from
the sun) The seeds have begun to sprout and the vines have
grown. She smiles and tends to them. She puts her head down
and continues to work.

Loung notices the change of rice fields.

EXT. RO LEAP DINING HALL - EVENING

Social contact among the new people is almost nonexistent.
Everyone keeps to themselves, fearing that if they share
personal thoughts or feelings someone will report them to the
Angkar.

Loung and Chou sits in silence. She looks at her food. The
rations are less.

Loung notices the man who had been tied to the tree
VICTIM/INFORMANT. His body language catches her eye. He is
humble but close to the KR. Giving information.

They seem to be talking about Pa. This makes Loung very
uncomfortable.

EXT. RO LEAP STREAM - DAY

Loung's POV of cows moving though the river. We reveal she is
in the river. Loung, Chou and the other girls wash their
clothes in a nearby stream. Without detergent they are never
very clean.

Loung looks at another group of older women down the stream.
She sees Ma who gives her a secret smile. DAVI catches her
eye. Despite the war and the famine, Davi's body is that of
a young woman. Her hair is cut short, but is thick and curly
and frames her small, oval face nicely. Loung stares at her
large, round brown eyes with their long lashes.

Davi sees her and shyly looks away.

Loung smiles at Keav who playfully splashes her with water.
Loung splashes back.

OMITTED - NOW SCENE 132A

EXT. RO LEAP - DUSK

MONSOON #1

Months have passed. Loung is out looking at the clouds. Loung and Chou are washing their hair and scrubbing their bodies by the side of their hut.

Loung notices three KR walk to Davi's family's hut and tell her parents they needed Davi to be the wife of a handicapped soldier. Davi's mother cries and wraps her arms around her daughter.

> DAVI'S MOTHER
> Take me. Davi is a lazy girl. Take
> me.

Davi cries harder at their words and clung desperately to her mother. Loung is too frightened to move.

> DAVI'S FATHER
> (on his knees)
> Please. Not my daughter. Please.

The KR grab Davi by her arms and pull her from her mother's shaking hug. Davi sobs loudly, begging them to let her stay but the KR drag her on. Her mother falls to her knees, palms together, and pleads with them not to take her only daughter. The father, still on his knees, lowers his head to the ground, banging his forehead on the dirt, and also pleading with the KR.

As they take her away, Davi turns around many times to see both her parents still on the ground, palms together, praying for her. She looks back until she can see them no more. Loung focus on Davi's father and the pain in his eyes.

INT. RO LEAP HUT - NIGHT

Loung sits still as Keav combs her hair. She watches as Meng and Kim play with Geak.

EXT. RO LEAP GARDEN - MORNING

Loung and the others arrive to see all vegetables have been taken from the ground. She watches as the chlops carry them away in crates. She and Chou begin again to prepare the land for the next crop. She looks over at Davi's sister.

INT. RO LEAP HUT - MORNING

Everyone is up early. Loung notices Khouy who seems upset.
She notices Pa and Meng having a serious private talk. Ma
packs Keav's black pyjama pants and shirt in a scarf. Keav
sits next to Ma with their hands touching. Loung is trying
to understand what is happening.

EXT. RO LEAP - DAY

Quietly Loung walks with her family to the town square where
other teenagers and families have already gathered. Other
teenagers have tears in their eyes as do their distraught
parents. Loung now understands.

Meng musses Loung's hair and gives her a smile. Loung watches
as the Village Chief calls them out and the base people hand
out tools and give them a plot number.

                    RO LEAP KHMER ROUGE LEADER
          The revolution is not taking place
          in this village alone; it is taking
          place throughout all of Kampuchea.
          Angkar needs strong young men and
          women. The Angkar knows what is
          best. We must trust in Angkar.

She watches as Khouy and Meng steal glances at Pa as they get
in line and begin to move off.

Keav and Ma wish they could embrace. They look into each
others eyes. Both full of tears. In a matter of minutes, the
chlops lead the children away while the families watch in
quiet despair.

Keav looks to Loung who tries to muster a smile, then she
hugs Pa and walks away in her black shirt and pants that are
frayed at the hem.

Loung watches Keav as she follows the soldiers, with twenty
other boys and girls, never looking back. Chou and Loung
watch with tears in their eyes and watch until Keav's figure
is no longer in sight.

OMITTED

INT. RO LEAP HUT - NIGHT

Loung watches Chou sleeping. She looks over at the empty place where Meng, Khouy and Keav used to sleep. Tears fall from her big brown eyes.

> PA
> Angkar is right. Soon the country
> will be prosperous. Angkar will
> take care of them.

Loung is confused, then hears footsteps. She looks through the slats to see two Chlops walking away. She looks to Pa. Silently they express the understanding.

EXT. RO LEAP - RIVER - DAY

END OF MONSOON #1

Loung, Chou and other girls walk in line to get water. Each balancing two water pails on a long flat piece of wood over their shoulders. They approach the water when, a stench attacks Loung's nose and she begins to cough. Coming around the path into a clearing, she knows what the smell is before she even spots the body. The corpse lies decomposing in the sun. She holds her breath and walk toward it.

> CHOU
> Let's go

Loung waves her hand at Chou and proceeds forward while she stays back. Pinching her nose, she approaches it. (Possibly face down but gun shots to make clear executed)

Black hair sinks into the grass, becoming one with the dirt. The chest cavity is caved in beneath the black clothes, home to hundreds of the black-green flies feasting on the body. Loung covers her mouth to push down vomit, not daring to look anymore. Quickly, she turns and walks away, but the smell of death still clings to her clothes.

> CHOU (CONT'D)
> What are you doing?

                    LOUNG
          Trying to loosen the body to float
          down stream.

Loung removes her pails, and with her stick helps to push the
body away. With the two of them beating on it, it bobs and
sways even more. Finally they loosen the leg and the body
floats a few feet down before getting stuck again near the
bank. This time he is inches away from them.

                    LOUNG (CONT'D)
          On three.

After a concerted effort, the body finally floats down the
river, his long hair spreading around. They wait a few
minutes until they believe the body fluids have all floated
past them before fetching the water. They move up stream for
a clean area.

EXT. RO LEAP DINING HALL - DAY

Rain falls. Loung and Chou line up with soup bowls in hand
along with the other girls to receive their rations. The
cooks used to serve them rice gruel, but now there are only
enough grains in the pot to make soup. (the soup is now very
clear)

When it's Loung's turn to receive the food, she watches
anxiously as the cook stirs the rice soup. Staring at the
rice pot, she lets out a breath of hopelessness when she sees
the lady take the ladle and stir the soup. Both hands tightly
gripping her bowl, Loung takes her two ladle fulls and walks
to a spot away from all the others.

Loung sits quietly, savoring it spoonful by spoonful,
drinking the broth first. What's left at the bottom of her
bowl is approximately three spoonfuls of rice, and she has to
make this last. She eats the rice slowly. Tears mix with the
food in her mouth. Her heart falls to her stomach when all
the eight grains are gone and she sees that the others are
still eating theirs.

She studies them. Everyone is thinner. They look like the
walking dead.

INT. RO LEAP HUT - NIGHT

Loung can't sleep. She looks at Chou. How her face has
changed.

Loung hears movement. She looks over in the direction of her
parents. She sees her father caressing her mother. She has
never seen them in such an intimate way before. She feels she
should look away but it warms her to see how Pa loves Ma. He
kisses her neck. (Not sex. Just affection. All very subtle so
nothing would be noticed by guards passing by.)

EXT. RO LEAP - DAY

Standing in the rows of ripe red bell peppers, tomatoes, and
green cucumbers, the sun burns hot on Loung's skin, drenching
her clothes.

In the next field over, Kim wipes his forehead and continues
his work in silence. As her fingers pluck the green beans,
Loung's mouth waters. Feeling the fuzzy hair of the beans
between her thumb and finger, she craves to put it in her
mouth.

Loung hears yelling. Chou is suddenly being questioned.

She reveals a bean in her hands half eaten. She begs for
forgiveness as tears roll down her face. Loung studies her
sister. She has never seen her like this. Her heart breaks
for her.

EXT. RO LEAP - DAY

On the way back from work, in line with the other girls,
Loung reaches for Chou's hand. She holds it for a moment
sending her a silent message.

Loung's POV of Pa working.

EXT. RO LEAP WELL - MORNING

DRY SEASON #2

A distorted image of Loung.

Loung is looking at her reflection in a pond. She has not
seen herself since Phnom Penh. The blurred child stares back
at her. She touches her face knowing how much it has changed.

She is always so tired. Starvation has done terrible things
to her body. Her body is thin all over, except for her
stomach and her feet. She lifts up her shirt and counts every
rib in her rib cage. Her stomach protrudes outward, bloated
like a ball between her chest and hips.

She looks at her feet. Calloused and dirty.

Loung and Chou roam the area for beetles, and crickets. Loung
catches a beetle and eats it. They pick up a handful of dirt
each, sift it in their hands as the big pebbles rise. They
take out the big pebbles and eat the rest of the dirt

Loung tilts her face up to the sky, forcing herself to look
directly into the sun. The brightness stings her eyes making
her temporarily blind.

EXT. RO LEAP - LATE DAY

The blue sky. Loung's POV.

DRY SEASON

Loung notices the leaves have shriveled and the trees brown.
People transporting dead bodies along the principal road to
the village to bury behind the village. They transport in a
very old mat or braided bamboo. One or two people follow the
body with a pickaxe.

A child cries in front of his house. Thin people work here
and there like zombies.

Under the summer sun, the stench of death is so strong in the
village, Loung covers her nose and mouth with her hands and
breathe only the air that filters through her fingers. The
neighbors are too weak to bury all the corpses. Some bodies
of recently dead lay waiting to be taken away. A very skinny
dog looks hungrily at the flesh. The smell permeates the
surrounding air.

She watches as the bodies are collected. Loung has seen the
ritual performed so many times that she now feels nothing.

A KR walks by and gives her a stern look. She stares back.

INT. RO LEAP HUT - NIGHT

Loung lies on her mat. She watches as Pa puts a few spoon fulls of uncooked rice in the secret rice bag. He puts the bag, inside a container, and hides it beneath a small pile of clothes so that the other villagers cannot see it.
PA watches three Chlops passing by on the main road of the village before hiding the rice.

INT. RO LEAP HUT - NIGHT

LOUNG'S DREAM (KUBRICK STYLE- CENTERED AND COLORFUL)

The shadow of a KR looking towards Loung like in the previous scene.

Loung is sitting alone at a long table. The table is covered with all of her favorite food in the world. There is food everywhere as far as her eyes can see! Red and crispy roasted pig, brown and golden duck, steaming dumplings, plump fried shrimp, and all kinds of sweet cakes! Everything looks so real. She shoves everything into her mouth at once with both hands, licking her fingers deliciously.

Yet the more she eats the hungrier she becomes. She eats with great anxiety and urgency, fearing the Khmer Rouge soldiers will come and take it all away from her. She is so greedy, she does not want to share the food with anyone. She sees shadows. She gorges and hides foods.

LOUNG'S DREAM ENDS

INT. RO LEAP HUT - 2 AM

Loung lays awake. Her stomach pains with hunger. She slowly, quietly, gets up and goes over the others sleeping bodies to get to the container. With her heart pounding, she slowly lifts off the top. Her hand reaches in and takes out a handful of uncooked rice (or snails or crickets) and quickly shoves it into her hungry mouth before anyone wakes and makes her put it back. Afraid that the crunch of uncooked rice might wake the others, she softens the grains with saliva. When it's soft enough, her teeth grinds the rice grains, producing a sweet taste that slowly down her throat. She wants more but stops herself.

INT. RO LEAP HUT - 6 AM

                    KIM
        Pa, someone was in the container
        last night.

Pa checks the container. He considers--

                    PA
        Maybe some rats got into it.

Pa wraps it up tight and moves it higher.

Pa looks at Loung. Shame burns her hand like a hot iron. As
if to rescue her, Geak wakes up and her cries of hunger
interrupt the incident. The guilt weighs heavily on Loung.

EXT. RO LEAP HUT - 6:10 AM

Loung keeps to herself washing food bowls in a bucket in
front of the hut.

Geak walks up to Loung and tugs at her clothes. Loung gently
pushes her away. Geak tries again. She wants Loung to pick
her up. Loung moves away from Geak.

Pa walks out of the hut on his way to work.

Chou comes over to help Loung. Kim walks by and intentionally
knocks against Loung as he passes on his way to work. She
looks up and he gives her a look. He knows.

Loung's lips quiver with shame. Chou grabs her hand.

EXT. RO LEAP - EARLY MORNING

Loung and Chou walk in line with others towards the garden.

INT. RO LEAP HUT - NIGHT

That night, Loung stares at Ma as she boils water for tea. She remembers that Ma used to be so beautiful. Now red lips are purple and dry, her cheeks are sunken, there are deep shadows under her eyes, her porcelain white skin is brown and wrinkled from the sun. Loung looks into her tea.

EXT. RO LEAP - EARLY MORNING

A beautiful orange sun rises.

EXT. RO LEAP HUT - EARLY MORNING

DRY SEASON BEFORE MONSOON #2

Early morning as everyone gets ready to report for work. Loung and Chou return to the hut with the water buckets. Ma sits on the porch combing Geak's hair and looking for lice. She washes her when the water arrives.

Loung watches Pa head out to work. A GIRL arrives in the village. She shows her pass to a chlop. She speaks to some people and is guided towards the Loung's family hut.

Loung watches as she comes closer. She seems concerned.

> GIRL
> I've come with a message from Comrade Keav.

The family gathers to listen. Ma shifts Geak on her hip.

                    GIRL (CONT'D)
          She has been sick. You are
          permitted to visit.

OMITTED

EXT. RO LEAP - MORNING

Chou is left home with Geak. Loung watches Ma put the slip in
her pocket as she leads them toward the road.

INT. RUN DOWN HOSPITAL - DAY

Ma guides Loung into the (pagoda or school turned into a
makeshift-) hospital. The sounds of suffering overwhelm her.
The room is full of patients. Most alone. One young boy
already dead.

Loung is just tall enough to see over the beds. She notices
coke bottles used as IV drips.

Splatter of blood on the floor catches Loung's attention. A
nurse pushes past her. Across the room Loung recognizes Keav.
Loung is almost too afraid to walk forward.

When Loung and Ma appear they see there seems to be no flesh
left on Keav's body. Keav's eyes are sunken deep into their
sockets, and she can hardly open them to look at her. When
she first sees Ma she does not recognize her. Keav wheezes
and gasps for air just from trying to talk to her. Ma breaks
down and weeps.

Keav keeps asking for Pa. She is so weak she cannot raise her
hand to wave the (CG) flies away from her face. She is so
dirty. They didn't even clean up her mess up. They just let
her lie there in her sickness and dirty sheets. Ma gets upset
and tries to help clean her. Loung looks to her sister. The
sight of her is terrifying.

EXT. RO LEAP GARDEN - DAY

Days later. Clouds in the sky. (Land is wet from 167-172,
sometimes rain). Loung and Chou work the land.

Loung sees the GIRL who came with a message about Keav. She watches from a distance as she is led to Ma in the fields. Loung looks on as her mother notices the girl and braces herself for the news.

We can tell from the body language that Keav has died. With the KR watching neither Ma nor Loung or Chou can express their grief.

INT. RO LEAP HUT - NIGHT

The hut is silent. Grief hangs heavy. Ma quietly making tea. Pa sitting alone. (Possibly carving for Chou, Loung and Kim) Loung and Chou whisper before bed.

>   LOUNG
> What happens when people die?

>   CHOU
> First they sleep peacefully not
> knowing they are dead. They sleep
> for three days and then on the
> third day they wake up. That's when
> they realize they are dead. Then
> they walk to a river, wash the dirt
> off their bodies, and start their
> journey to heaven to wait for their
> next life.

>   LOUNG
> When will they come back?

>   CHOU
> I don't know.

>   LOUNG
> I hope she won't come back here.

EXT. RO LEAP STREAM - DAY

Chou and Loung are at the stream doing laundry. They are surrounded by other girls doing the same. No splashing or laughter now. Only silence. Like Loung and Chou, the children are so starved they hardly have the energy to wash the clothes.

EXT. RO LEAP - DAY

BEFORE DRY SEASON.

Base children play. Loung feels hate for them.

The air is hotter and drier now. Time passes slowly. Loung and Chou eat lunch huddled together. The food rations have reduced even more.

The man with the Birthmark (who was tied to the tree) is speaking with a Chlop. Loung notices as they give Pa a look. Pa lowers his head.

                    LOUNG
          I'm going to kill them one day.

She looks back and sees Chou smiling to herself.

                    LOUNG (CONT'D)
          You don't think I can? I can.

                    CHOU
               (simply)
          I don't want you to. I don't want
          anyone to kill (hurt) anyone.

Chou looks sad.

INT. RO LEAP HUT - NIGHT

                    MA
               (panicked)
          How would they know?

Lying on her back next to Chou and Kim, Loung pretends to be asleep.

                    PA
          Someone probably denounced me.

                    MA
          How is it possible? We hid our
          names. Everything.

Loung rolls over to her side. Ma and Pa become quiet, waiting for her to go back to sleep. Staring at Kim's back, Loung forces herself to breathe regularly. Pa whispers something we can not hear.

                    MA (CONT'D)
               (whispering)
          No. Please. They are too young.
          They cannot defend themselves.

Pa takes a deep breath.

                    PA
          Not now then, but soon.

Geak kicks and moans in her sleep. Ma picks her up and puts her down between Pa and herself. Loung rolls over once more, this time facing Chou's back. She spies Ma and Pa asleep facing each other on their sides with Geak in the middle, their hands touching above Geak's head.

EXT. RO LEAP HUT - LATE DAY

The next evening, while sitting with Kim outside on the steps of their hut (sweeping). Loung looks out at the camp, and up to the sky. When Loung focuses her eyes back on the earth, she sees two men in black walking towards her with their rifles casually hanging on their backs.

                KHMER ROUGE WITH RIFLE
     Is Comrade Nath here?

                KIM
     Yes comrade.

Pa hears them and comes out of the hut, his body rigid as our
family gathers around him.

                PA
     Comrades, what can I do for you?

                KHMER ROUGE WITH RIFLE
     We need your help to repair the
     bridge near Prey Svay. Come with us
     Comrade.

                PA
     Could you please wait a moment so
     that I can pack my things?

The soldiers nod to Pa. Pa and Ma go inside the hut.

Loung stares at a dirty ax hanging on the side of the
soldiers belts. There is something on it. It could be dirt it
could be blood. There is also rope on the belt of one KR. The
soldier smiles at her. Loung looks away.

She notices the Man with the birthmark. He looks guilty and
turns back into his hut.

Loung moves to the wall and looks through the slats in the
wall. She sees her father embracing her mother in a way she
has never seen. So deeply loving and intimate. She holds him
so tight as if she could keep him with her forever if only
she never let go. (To discuss what he packs and what he
leaves behind. Possibly a strand of Keav's hair)

Tears fall from her face. Pa wipes her tears and lifts her
head. He needs her to be strong. He gives her one last kiss.

Loung looks away. Her focus returns to the soldiers in front
of her.

Moments later, Pa comes out alone. Inside, Loung hears Ma
sobbing quietly. Opposite the soldiers, Pa straightens his
shoulders, and for the first time since the Khmer Rouge
takeover, he stands tall. Thrusting out his chin and holding
his head high.

Looking up at him, Loung sees his chest inflates and exhales
deeply, and his jaw is square as he clenches his teeth.
Loung reaches up her hand and lightly tugs at his pants leg.
Pa puts his hand on her head and tousles her hair.

Suddenly he surprises her and picks her up off the ground.
His arms tight around her, Pa holds her and kisses her hair.

Loung's feet dangling in the air, she squeezes her eyes shut
and wrap her arms around his neck, not wanting to let go.

>   PA (CONT'D)
>   (whispers)
>   My beautiful girl.

His lip quivers into a small smile.

Pa puts Loung down. He walks slowly to Chou and takes Geak
from her arms. Looking into her face, he cradles her and
gently rocks her back and forth before bending and gathering
Chou into his arms also. His head high and his chest puffed
out like a small man, Kim walks over to Pa and stands quietly
next to him. Letting go of Chou and Geak, Pa stoops down and
lays both hands on Kim's shoulders. As Kim's face crumbles,
Pa's face is rigid and calm.

>   PA (CONT'D)
>   Look after your Ma and your sisters
>   and yourself.

Pa walks away with a soldier on either side of him. Loung
stands and waves to him. She watches Pa's figure get smaller
and smaller, and still she waves to him, hoping he will turn
around and wave back. He never does. She watches until his
figure disappears into the horizon. When she can no longer
see Pa, Loung turns around and goes.

Loung looks inside their hut, where Ma sits in the corner of
the room crying.

In her heart she knows the truth, but her mind cannot accept
the reality of what this all means. Loung watches as Chou and
Kim go to her to ask what has happened.

OMITTED

INT. RO LEAP HUT - NIGHT

Loung lies on her back. Outside the wind blows in the
branches, and the leaves rustle and sing to each other. The
clouds part, and the moon and stars shine and give life to
the darkness. Time stands still this night.

IMAGES IN LOUNG'S HEAD AS SHE IMAGINES WHAT HAPPENED TO HER
FATHER-

EXT. FOREST - NIGHT

A dark hole in the ground. There are already many dead people in the mass grave, their bodies sprawled on top of each other. Their black pajama clothes are soaked with blood.

A soldier leads a man to the edge of the hole, his arms tied behind his back. It's Pa. The soldier pushes on Pa's shoulders, making him kneel. The soldier has blindfolded him. Pa prays silently. The soldier raises the ax above his head. Pa is killed.

INT. RO LEAP HUT - NIGHT

Tears fall from Loung's eyes.

She slides next Chou. Beside them, Kim holds on tight to Geak.

Loung's mind swirls with pain and anger. The pain spasm convulses as if it is eating away her linings. Turning on her side, she digs her hands into her stomach and squeezes it violently to make the physical pain stop. Then the sadness surrounds her. Dark and black it looms over her, pulling her deeper and deeper into it. HER EYES GROW COLD.

She can still hear the faint noise of Ma's muffled cries outside, but now does not feel her pain. She is becoming numb.

INT. RO LEAP HUT - MORNING

Ma is up before anyone else the next morning. Her face is all puffy, her eyes are red and swollen shut.

Loung watches as Ma folds Pa's clothes and puts them and his few other belongings in a loving pile and tucks them away. She notices Kim. He helps Geak change. He is different somehow. As if he now knows he must be the man of the house. He straightens up as if making the decision. The loudspeakers announces. Loung watches Kim walk to work.

EXT. RO LEAP - EARLY MORNING

DRY SEASON

Ma and the other women harvest the rice.

EXT. RO LEAP CORNFIELD - MORNING

Stalks of corn in the sunlight. Loung looks over at Kim who is nearby working with the other young boys. He looks at the men guarding the corn. He watches as they stand nearby enjoying cigarettes.

One Chlop looks at Loung. She stares back defiantly. He only winks, making it worse.

INT. RO LEAP HUT - NIGHT

Loung watches- Kim won't hear no. He is determined. He takes a krama and heads out the door. Chou and Loung don't try to stop him. They watch as he goes.

Ma looks afraid. She doesn't move.

Later-

Kim is still not back. (Find a visual way to show passage of time.) Loung looks to Ma who is holding Geak for comfort. Chou sits in the corner of the room, staring out into her own world.

Suddenly Kim climbs into the hut. He is smiling and carrying a bag of fresh corn. Loung rushes to help him carry it into the house. Seeing Kim, Ma puts Geak down so she can greet him. They stay very quiet so not to attract attention.

Loung edges herself closer and closer to the bags of corn. Her nose inhales the aroma. Her eyes fixate on the yellow ears.

                    MA
              (to herself)
          They have turned us into thieves.

Loung hears this but can't listen. Her stomach is too empty to feel anything but happy for the food.

EXT. RO LEAP - NIGHT

(discuss how it is cooked) The clouds are moving furiously fast, blocking any moonbeams from touching the earth. Ma passes around the corn. Kim plays with Geak who seems a bit livelier.

Later- Ma tells a story as she combs knots out of Geak's hair.

She tells the story. She smiles at Kim. The story is for him. Loung and Ma share a smile. It's been a while since she has felt that connection.

INT. RO LEAP HUT - NIGHT

The following night, Loung watches Kim sling a bag (or scarf) over his shoulders and climb down the steps of the hut.

His knees buckle when he reaches the ground. Quickly, he straightens himself before anyone notices.

Loung grabs a bag, slings it over her shoulder and follows behind him.

EXT. RO LEAP - NIGHT

The sky is very dark.

His small feet carry him into the darkness. Kim looks behind him frightened upon hearing a noise. He breathes a deep sigh of relief when he realizes it's Loung. He gestures for her to stay quiet.

EXT. RO LEAP CORNFIELD - CONTINUOUS

Then he sees the field ahead of him. It is thick with stalks of corn, each with three or four ears, standing twice the size of the small boy. His eyes scan the area all around him.

Kim runs from his hiding place into the cornfield. His fingers work busily to fill the bags.

Loung comes closer.

Suddenly, two hands grab Kim from behind and throw him to the ground. He tries to get back on his feet. Through her hiding place in the field, Loung sees two Khmer Rouge, their rifles slung across their backs. One soldier grabs Kim by the arm and pulls him off the ground, but his knees buckle. His head spins. He is shaking with terror. A hand slaps him hard on the face. The pain is sharp and cutting, but he bites his jaws together to stop its hurt.

> KR
> How dare you steal from Angkar.
> Thief!

They yell at him, but he is too stunned to hear them. More hands push him down. He is on all fours now and following their orders when a hard-booted foot kicks him in the stomach, knocking his breath away. He is in the mud again, gasping for breath.

LOUNG is frozen with fear. She desperately wants to run to her brother but she can't. She stares, unable to look away.

Another foot stomps on his back and pushes his face into the mud. He opens his mouth, gasping for air, but instead chokes on a mouthful of mud. He is sick with terror, and he does not know what to do next. A hand pulls him up by the hair and a soldier is staring at him.

> KR (CONT'D)
> Are you going to steal again?

> KIM
> No comrade.

Kim whimpers as blood drips out of his mouth. But that isn't enough for them. More hands and more legs continue their assault on him. The same questions are asked of him and the same answer is given.

Then one takes his rifle off his shoulder and points it at him. Kim cries, tears pouring out.

> KIM (CONT'D)
> (trembling)
> Please. Please don't kill me.

One laughs at him. He is no longer a boy trying to be the man of the house. He is just a twelve-year-old boy now, looking into the barrel of a rifle.

> KIM (CONT'D)
> Please comrade. Please don't kill
> me. I will never do it again.
> Please.

He turns the rifle around and smashes its butt into Kim's skull. The soldier pushes Kim with his rifle as if telling him to move.

> KR
> (with warning)
> Those who steal anything from the community are enemies. No gain in keeping, no loss in weeding out. Next time I will kill you. Go.

Kim rises unsteadily to his feet and limps home.

Loung trails very slowly, quietly behind.

EXT. RO LEAP HUT - NIGHT

Loung sees Ma put her hands over her mouth to stifle a scream. Against the backdrop of the dark, she sees Kim's twelve-year-old body. In his hand are two empty bags. Ma sees the unmistakable color of blood on his clothes and marks on his muddy face. His eyes are half closed, he is shaken, but he does not cry. Ma rushes over to him and gently touches his wounded face. She cries over his cut swollen lips and cringes as she touches the blood dripping from his skull.

> MA
> My poor little boy, my poor little boy. Look what they have done to you. My poor little boy.

INT. RO LEAP HUT - NIGHT

Kim is quiet and does not resist Ma's help taking off his bloody shirt. Chou bites her lip at seeing her brother's body so badly beaten. Raw, red marks and painful bruises are everywhere on his rib cage and back. Geak begins to cry. Loung stands in the corner with more conviction than ever to kill these soldiers, to avenge the blood that drips from her brother's skull.

Kim does not cry. He flinches when Ma puts a wet rag on his bruised and bleeding head. (This time seeing a deep wound, Loung doesn't look away. She stares at it, following the blood from the gash down to the small puddle on the floor)

Ma lays Kim down, he closes his eyes, and falls asleep.

LATER—

Fearing he might die and Loung will not know about it, she walks over to him every few minutes and puts her hand under his nose to feel his breath.

EXT. RO LEAP GARDEN - DAY

The children work in the garden. Loung looks across to the area where Kim is. His wounds are almost healed. He is now more withdrawn. She looks at him he looks like the little boy that he is. She feels for him.

INT. RO LEAP HUT - EVENING

Loung is focused on Geak. (possibly brushing her hair and looking for lice) Noticing how frail she is.

Ma returns from work. She gathers Kim, Chou, and Loung together. With all of them sitting in a circle waiting for her, Ma nervously walks around the hut outside to make sure no one can hear. When she joins her children, her eyes are filled with tears.

>   MA
> You three have to leave and go far
> away. You will go in different
> directions. Kim, to the south; Chou
> north; and Loung east. Walk until
> you come to a work camp. Tell them
> you are orphans and they will take
> you in. Change your names. Don't
> even tell each other your new
> names. Don't let people know who
> you are.

Ma's voice grows stronger with determination as the words pour out.

>   MA (CONT'D)
> This way if they catch you, they
> cannot get to the rest because you
> will have no information to give
> them.

Her mouth says many more words, but Loung cannot hear them. Fear creeps its way into her body, making it tremble.

>   LOUNG
> I don't want to go.

                          MA
            You have no choice.

Loung is too shocked to speak.

OMITTED

INT. RO LEAP HUT - NIGHT

Loung watches as Ma packs their things.

Chou and Kim are dressed and ready to go. Chou hugging Geak.

Ma packs Loung's one pair of clothes, wraps food bowl in a scarf, and ties it diagonally around her back.

EXT. RO LEAP HUT - NIGHT

Slowly Loung climbs down the steps to where Chou and Kim are waiting for her.

                          MA
            Remember, don't go together and
            don't come back.

Loung's heart sinks as she realizes Ma really is sending them away.

                          LOUNG
            I'm not going.

Loung plants her feet to the ground, refusing to move.

                          MA
            Yes, you are. I don't want you
            here.

                          LOUNG
            I'm not going.

                          MA
            I cannot take care of all you kids.
            You are too much work for me. I
            WANT you to leave.

Ma stares at them blankly. Loung's arms reach out for Ma pleading with her to take her into her arms. But she swats Loung back with a quick slap.

                          MA (CONT'D)
            Now go.

She turns Loung around by the shoulders and bends down to give her a hard swat on the butt, pushing her away.

Kim is already walking away from them with his eyes looking ahead and his back rigid. Chou follows slowly behind him, her sleeves continuously wiping her eyes. Reluctantly, Loung drags herself away from Ma and catches up with them. After a few steps, she turns around and sees that Ma has already gone back into the hut. Geak sits at the door, watching them leave. She lifts her hand and waves to Loung. Loung can't bring herself to wave back.

EXT. ROAD - MORNING

The three siblings walk in silence.

OMITTED

EXT. ROAD - DAY

Hours later -

The sun climbs to the backs of their heads, scorching them. It is time for Kim to go off on his own path. He stops his sisters and again repeats Ma's instructions without emotion. Without words of good-bye or good luck, he turns and walks away. Loung doesn't know if or when she will ever see him again. With her hands clenched into fists by her sides, she stands there and her eyes follow his body until she can no longer see him.

Chou and Loung look at the fork in the road. They stand for a while before they decide they cannot separate themselves so they head off in the same direction. (Chou will find Loung's hand and pull her gently with her.)

EXT. ROAD - DAY

Loung and Chou walk in silence all through the morning as the sun beats down on them. Their eyes look everywhere for signs of human life but find none. All around them, the trees are brown, their green leaves, wilted in the heat of the white sky, hanging quietly on the branches. The only sound comes from their feet and the pebbles that roll away from their toes.

Ahead of them Loung sees KR. Her heart begins to beat rapidly as they approach.

> LOUNG
> Comrade, we are orphans. We are looking for a place to live.

The soldier stares at her. She feels he knows she is lying. Finally he guides her.

> KR GUIDE
> This way for xxx turn right when you see a flag and follow the dirt path to the fields.

They thank him respectfully and move on.

EXT. ROAD - DAY

Chou and Loung pass the flag and follow the dirt trail winding and stretching before them. It is afternoon when they finally see a camp.

EXT. CHILDREN'S WORK CAMP - DAY

Loung looks at the camp. It consists of six huts. Opposite them are two open huts that are used as the communal kitchen and three smaller huts where the supervisors live. The camp is surrounded by rice fields on all sides. The children are harvesting. Another fifty children lined up at the wells are in the process of watering the gardens. Buckets of water are passed from one person to person, the last person with the bucket pours the water onto the garden and runs the bucket back to the well.

Standing at the front, Chou and Loung are greeted by the camp supervisor. MET BONG is as tall as Ma but much bigger and more intimidating. Her black hair is cut chin-length and square, the same style of all other KR women.

> MET BONG
> Comrade, what are you doing here?

> LOUNG
> Met Bong, my sister and I are orphans looking for a place to live.

> MET BONG
> How old are you?

58.

                    LOUNG
          I am seven. She is ten.

                    MET BONG
          Follow me.

EXT. CHILDREN'S WORK CAMP DINING AREA - EARLY EVENING

Loung and Chou line up with other girls. Loung is surprised
to see the food rations are much better. COCONUT CUTTING
GIRLS sit on mats preparing one for each workmate. She
watches as the food is put into her bowl. Then she and Chou
find a place to sit next to a sweet looking girl, NA, who
seems sad and alone.

EXT. CHILDREN'S WORK CAMP - MEETING ROOM - DUSK

Chou, Loung, Na, and others gather for nightly lessons.
Images of communist leaders hanging from the rafter. A
TEACHER reads the latest news or propaganda from the Angkar.

                    TEACHER
               (in a full voice)
          Angkar is all powerful! Angkar is
          the savior and liberator of the
          Khmer people. You are the children
          of Angkar. Long live the
          revolutionary Angkar!

Children clap, raise their fisted arms and scream "Cheyo!
Cheyo! Cheyo!" (Viva! Viva! Viva!) Loung and Chou follow
suit, though they do not understand the propaganda of what
Teacher is saying."

                    TEACHER (CONT'D)
          Only you children are free from
          stain. Clay is molded while it is
          soft. Today our soldiers at the
          front line crushed the Yuon enemies
          who try to devour our country.
          Cheyo/Viva our glorious
          revolutionary army of Kampuchea!

                    ALL GIRLS
               (fists in the air)
          Chevo! Chevo!

Anger builds inside Loung as she thinks of what Angkar and
the Khmer Rouge have done to her family.

INT. CHILDREN'S WORK CAMP - NIGHT

Loung and Chou are wedged closely together on a wooden bamboo plank with fifty other girls.

EXT. CHILDREN'S WORK CAMP RICE FIELDS - DAY

Loung and Chou now work in the rice fields with the other girls. Harvesting is hard work. Loung watches the others to learn what to do. Na helps her and shows her.

EXT. CHILDREN'S WORK CAMP

The girls return from work. VAN a girl around Chou's age and size makes herself known as a leader. She stares at Chou. She finds her sweet soft nature weak.

Van pushes into Chou on purpose. Chou is of such a gentle nature it really shocks her. She tries to move away from Van who gets near her and pushes her again. SAT, Van's friend is also there and giving Chou a hard time.

EXT. CHILDREN'S WORK CAMP

Another day working in the rice fields. Sweat pours down Loung's face. She looks over at Van who is saying things to Chou under her breath. Chou is trying to be strong.

INT. CHILDREN'S WORK CAMP - NIGHT

Chou and Loung hold each other as they sleep on the wood boards surrounded by all the other girls.

INT. CHILDREN'S WORK CAMP - EARLY EVENING

While washing up for dinner one evening, Van, walks up and pinches Chou's arm. She leans in and whispers something cruel.

As if possessed by a will of their own, Loung's arms reach for her neck and her hands close around the girls throat, squeezing hard. Van's face turns white with confusion. She gasps for air, chokes under the pressure of Loung's fingers. She grabs Loung's arms, her nails scratching her skin. Loung refuses to let go. Sharp pain explodes on Loung's shin as Van kicks her. Loung lunges at her with her body, knocking her to the ground. Sitting on her chest, Loung's eyes pierce hers. Her hands slap Van's face.

Loung is pushed to the ground by Met Bong.

                    MET BONG
          Enough!

She points to Van.

MET BONG (CONT'D)
Go and wash up. (to Loung) You will
water the garden tonight. No
dinner. And no sleep until you
finish.

Met Bong instructs another girl to guard Loung and make sure
she does as she is told.

As Loung struggles to get up, the crowd around her slowly
dissipates. Chou looks down, unable to help. She grabs the
water pail to start to water the garden.

EXT. CHILDREN'S WORK CAMP GARDEN - EARLY EVENING TO NIGHT

Loung works while the girls eat their dinner, recite
propaganda at the nightly lessons (in the school room if
nearby), and get ready to go to bed. She does not cry,
scream, or beg for mercy.

Many hours into the night, Met Bong approaches and tells her
to go to sleep. Without looking at her, Loung drops her pail
and walks in her hut.

OMITTED

EXT. CHILDREN'S WORK CAMP - MORNING

MONSOON SEASON BEGINS

Loung works the field with other girls.

Months have passed and with increased food rations Loung and
Chou are still slim but they have grown stronger and seem
healthier.

Loung's feet in the muddy water, Loung's ankles and toes
start to itch. She lifts one foot out of the water and
reacts. There are fat black leeches on her ankles.

Loung pulls out a stalk of grass. Her hands hold both ends
of the stalk, and she swipes the grass down and around her
ankle. The leeches fall off onto the ground, leaving her
ankle bleeding.

She ties her pants tight around her ankles.

From afar, Met Bong screams for her.

Chou now works in the kitchen. Loung sees her as she passes
and reports to Met Bong.

                    MET BONG
              (to Loung with elation)
          You should be happy with yourself.
          The camp you are going to is for
          stronger children. There you will
          be trained and help to fight the
          war.

Loung tries to absorb what has just been told to her.

EXT. CHILDREN'S WORK CAMP - MORNING

At the break of dawn, Loung packs her clothes and food bowl. Hooking their elbows together Chou and Loung walk towards Met Bong.

The girls hug wrapping their arms tightly around each other. Loung can feel Chou's tears wet her hair. Met Bong announces it is time for everyone to move. (discuss other ways to show affection that are more suitable under KR)

Chou refuses to let go of Loung's hand. With all her strength Loung pulls her hand away and moves to catch up with the others. She can't look back. Loung holds back her tears and lifts her head bracing herself for what's to come.

EXT. CHILD SOLDIER TRAINING CAMP - DAY

Met Bong leads Loung and two others to another camp a half an hour's walk away. When they arrive, Loung notices in many ways it seems similar in set up to the old camp. Met Bong passes them off to MET SREI. (Try a full camp bokotor training as the new girls arrive.)

The new work camp is surrounded by forest. All around are hammocks in tall palm trees that sway lightly in the wind. Some boys are training. One looks at her and smiles, SMILING BOY. He looks about twelve years old, has a round face, black wavy hair, and a small, dark sinewy body.

This familiar gesture of human friendship is one that she has become so unused to. She smiles slightly and turns her attention back to the camp.

The camp is made up of about ninety girls and boys, their ages ranging from Nine to fifteen. Loung is one of the younger ones.
In this camp I suggest to have 2 groups of children, gathered according to their age. Met Srei manages the group of girls like Loung and a boy, Met Prem leads the unit of 13-16 boys - only boys.
There could be a unit of young boys too and a unit of young girls. But they all are separated when they sleep, when they eat...

EXT. CHILD SOLDIER TRAINING CAMP - NIGHT

Loung's first night at the camp, the two groups gather around a roaring bonfire to listen to the latest propaganda. Met Srei stands before them preaching the message.

                    MET SREI
          We owe everything to Angkar! We are
          strong because of the Angkar.

Loung joins the others in the obligatory fists in the air.

                    ALL
          Chevo! Chevo!

                    MET SREI
          Youns are like the devil and some
          refuse to die. We must use our
          knives and spill their insides into
          the dirt. Smash the Yuon agressors
          who devour our country! Down!

                    ALL
          Down! Down! Down! Baratchey!
          Brarchey!

As if possessed by powerful spirits, her arms shaking
furiously at the sky, their lips moving faster and faster as
she spits words about the glory of the Angkar and the
unbeatable Khmer soldiers. The children's furor matches that
of the Met Srei's.

                    MET SREI
          Long live the courageous,
          invincible Revolutionary Army of
          Kampuchea.

                    ALL
          Cheyo! Cheyo!

They thunder in appreciation. Loung looks at the sea of fists
in the air.

EXT. CHILD SOLDIER TRAINING CAMP - NIGHT

When the speeches are over, the circle opens up and the kids
gather to one side of the fire. Four boys get up from the
crowd, with mandolins and homemade drums in hand. They stand
to the side of the crowd and start to play their instruments.
They beat the drums and strum the mandolins while their feet
tap the ground.

Five girls walk up to the front and stand facing the crowd.
All are wearing beautiful black shirts and pants, not the
faded, gray-black Loung has on, but shiny and new, with
bright red scarves around their waists. They wear red
ribbons across their foreheads with red fake flowers made of
dyed straw. Forming a line, they sing and dance.

All the songs are about worshiping the powerful leader of the Angkar, Pol Pot, the glory of Angkar society, and the unbeatable Khmer soldiers.

Later-

They dance scenes depicting farmers at work, and a song about a woman soldier hiding her knife in her skirt and thrusting it into the heart of a Youn. It has been years since Loung has heard music.

Watching the girls sing and dance, a strange feeling comes over Loung. Though the words they sing describe images of blood and war, the girls smile. Their hands move gracefully in unison, their bodies sway and twirl to the rhythm of the music.

FLASHBACK - a traditional dance from before the war. Gold bracelets and headpieces glisten (Possibly also Chou dancing at home) - FLASHBACK ENDS

The dancing continues. Loung watches the girls full of grace and movement.

EXT. SOLDIER CAMP

Loung is given a new uniform and a hammock. She prepares for her first night alone.

EXT. CHILD SOLDIER TRAINING FIELDS - DAY

Loung wears a new soldier uniform and green cap on her first day of bokotor training. (kids nearby possibly sharpen sticks, she joins later in the day)

EXT. CHILD SOLDIER TRAINING CAMP - MORNING

DRY SEASON BEGINS

Loung trains bokotor. She is more used to it now and has gained a bit of weight.

She looks over and watches the boys bayonet fight training.

EXT. CHILD SOLDIER TRAINING CAMP - DAY

Depending on their size and age, the children are given
different jobs and training. Loung sits with a group of girls
sharpening sticks and building traps.

EXT. CHILD SOLDIER TRAINING CAMP - DUSK

The children are gathered around the fire. Loung stares at
the flames.

> TRAINING OFFICER
> It is very easy to train someone to
> use weapons but to train a mind is
> more difficult. You must follow
> orders without hesitation.

Loung looks at the faces of the other children listening.
Their big brown eyes glow by the light of the fire.

Met Srei leads the children in propaganda songs. Loung must
sing along.

INT. CHILD SOLDIER TRAINING CAMP - NIGHT

Loung climbs into her hammock. She looks around at the girls
she lives with. No one is a friend. No one can replace her
family. She sees two girls sleeping near each other. She
misses Chou.

EXT. CHILD SOLDIER TRAINING CAMP - DAY

The Smiling Boy is there and this time Loung smiles back.

Met Srei calls the other children to her. They all come
together in the center of the camp.

Met Srei stands up and disappears, only to return moments
later with an armful of tools. They clang noisily as she
drops them in a pile in front of them.

> MET SREI
> All these tools you already know.
> But in the hands of fighters, they
> are weapons of war. The machete
> cuts. The hammer smashes. (re the
> sickle) The point of the sickle can
> pierce a person's skull.

Met Srei picks a rifle from the pile, the same kind Loung has seen many times before on the shoulders of the Khmer Rouge soldiers.

>   MET SREI (CONT'D)
>   This weapon is very expensive. It
>   is easy to shoot.

Met Srei calls Loung up from the group. She puts the rifle on her small shoulder. Its butt digs into her chest.

Met Srei then instructs her to sling one arm over it, balancing its weight with her arm. Loung does this easily but against her will. She then takes the rifle and slips the strap on Loung's shoulder. The rifle hangs on her back a foot from the ground, its butt bouncing lightly on her calf.

Loung focuses on it, realizing that this is the weapon that made Kim bleed the same weapon that smashed into his skull. SHE HAS FLASHES OF THAT MEMORY. Her hand shakes slightly, but she steadies it by clutching the stock tightly until her knuckles turn white.

>   MET SREI (CONT'D)
>   Your extended left hand holds and
>   balances the rifle. Your right hand
>   aims and squeezes the trigger.

She calls each child one by one and teaches her how to hold the rifle. Loung watches.

EXT. CHILD SOLDIER TRAINING CAMP - DAY

Loung and others in a class to lay land mines.

She looks up and sees some of the boys gathered together as they march out of the camp and off to war. Smiling Boy is there. He's not smiling this time.

EXT. TREES - MORNING

Light shines through the trees. Suddenly we see movement. The girls appear and disappear as they practice manoeuvres.

OMITTED

EXT. CHILD SOLDIER TRAINING CAMP - NIGHT AM

Loung sits in fear.

The sky is dark and cloudless, allowing the full moon to
shine through, giving everything an eerie, silvery glow.

The cool wind blows quietly. All is quiet, except for the crickets.

The night sky looms ever more black in front of her. Something rustles loudly in the tall grass. She holds her breath and look around the compound. Her heart races. The tree trunks expand and contract as if they are breathing. The branches shake and swing, transform into hands. The grass sways like waves heading toward her.

Loung clutches her weapon to her chest. Her eyes scanning the trees.

EXT. CHILD SOLDIER TRAINING CAMP - MORNING

MONSOON SEASON

The ground is wet. The children train. The young girls, covered in muddy water run in patterns. It almost looks like they are playing but on closer investigation, they are being taught to run in zigzag lines when in battle. Being taught to dodge bullets. A comrade yells out and they all drop to the ground and begin to crawl forward. (Practice laying land mines or set traps)

As Loung crawls forward she has trouble seeing through all the mud on her face. She is yelled at and pushes forward.

EXT. CHILD SOLDIER TRAINING CAMP - DUSK

The rain falls on Loung as she and the other girls finish another hard day in the rain bokotor training.

INT. CHILD SOLDIER TRAINING CAMP - NIGHT

The hammocks swing in the wind and rain. Loung lays awake thinking of her family. She listens to the rain.

EXT. CHILD SOLDIER TRAINING CAMP - MORNING

DRY SEASON BEGINS.

The sun shines down on Loung who appears stronger. She and the other girls train with the few sickles, hoes, knives, stakes, and guns that are available in the camp.

Later –

The children eat together. At breakfast, Loung hides food in her scarf.

OMITTED

EXT. CHILD SOLDIER TRAINING CAMP

Loung's fingers tremble as she buttons her black shirt. She runs her fingers through her greasy hair to smooth it out.

OMITTED - CONTENT MERGED INTO SCENE 259

EXT. CHILD SOLDIER TRAINING CAMP - MORNING

Loung picks up her pass from Met Srei.

>   MET SREI
>   Spend a few hours with your sister
>   then come back immediately.

She walks out the gates of the camp.

EXT. ROAD - DAY

Following the same path she took a year ago, she walks back to Ro Leap. When she was last on this road she was a scared little kid. She is no longer that kid. (possibly passing the labour camp where Chou is or the area she separated from Kim)

EXT. RO LEAP - AFTERNOON

Finally Loung sees the village. It looks familiar yet it's changed. Seems there are less people and more starved around the huts. Too sick to work now. She stays low and in the shadows.

The town square is deserted and quiet as she crosses it to face the rows of huts. Her lungs expand and contract rapidly. She forces herself closer to their hut.

INT. RO LEAP HUT - AFTERNOON

Everything is still there. Their wooden rice bowls and spoons. Their pile of black clothes. Loung searches the hiding place. She finds Ma's blue shirt and the family photo wrapped inside.

                    LOUNG
          Ma!

Getting a bad feeling, Loung calls out again. No one replies. She notices a bowl knocked over. She puts it on the small shelf.

Davi's mother stands in the doorway of the next hut.

                    DAVI'S MOTHER
          They went with the soldiers.

The woman says quietly and looks away. She stares into the distance, refusing to look back at Loung. They both know what it means when the soldiers come to the village and take someone with them.

Loung stares into the empty hut. They cannot have survived three years of starvation and the loss of Keav and Pa only to be taken now! She fought so hard to live! She cannot be gone. Poor little Geak, she never got anything good out of life.

At the sound of a baby, Davi's mother leaves.

OMITTED

MEMORY of Ma singing her to sleep in Phnom Penh flashes before Loung.

She cannot be strong anymore. Tears run uncontrollably down her face. Her chest compresses, her insides gnaw at her, eating away at her sanity. She has to run away, she has to leave. Somehow her legs take over and carry her away from the village. Her body goes weak when she wonders which one the soldiers killed first...

HER MIND PROJECTS IMAGES OF THE TWO OF THEM TOGETHER. HER THOUGHTS OF WHAT MIGHT HAVE HAPPENED -

EXT. DARK FOREST - NIGHT (OR DAY) - TBD

Ma cries softly, her body tense with fear.

Suddenly the rattling sounds of the rifles go off and bullets pierce through bodies, silencing their screams.

Geak moves to Ma's slumped-over body with her face in the mud. Geak is too young to understand what has just happened. She calls Ma. She touches Ma's cheeks and ears, and grabs her hair to try to lift her face out of the mud, but she is not strong enough. While rubbing her eyes, she wipes Ma's blood all over her own face. She pounds her fists on Ma's back, trying to wake her up, but Ma is gone. Holding on to Ma's head, Geak screams and screams, not stopping to take in any air. Seconds later, a shot, Geak too is silenced.

OMITTED

EXT. RO LEAP - DUSK

Loung walks away from Ro Leap deafened by the ringing in her ears.

Tears pour from her as she drags herself away from the village. Her eyes flutter, it is as if she is drifting away into another place, into the deepest recesses of her mind to hide from the pain. Suddenly, the world becomes hazy and blurry. It is black all around her, soothing and empty.

EXT. CHILD SOLDIER TRAINING CAMP - MORNING

Staring straight ahead, Loung regains conscious thought. Slap. She is back at camp, standing before Met Srei. Her hand massages her stinging cheek; she tastes blood in her mouth.

> MET SREI
> (demanding)
> Where have you been?

For Loung, the world comes back into focus. He looks at the girls standing around staring.

> LOUNG
> I went to see my sister.

> MET SREI
> And stayed there for three days?

Loung's eyes widen in disbelief.

> LOUNG
> I don't know. I don't know where I
> was.

Met Srei slaps her again. Loung almost loses her balance. Met Srei screams into her face.

> MET SREI
> You won't tell me? No food tonight
> and I will reduce your ration until
> you do.

Met Srei walks away. After she is gone, Loung walks to the well and pull up a pail of water. Drinking some, pouring the rest over her feet. Rubbing one foot against the other, she removes the layers of red mud to expose her small, wrinkled toes.

OMITTED

EXT. CHILD SOLDIER TRAINING CAMP - MORNING

Remaining boys practice bokotor.

Early morning Met Srei takes her old clothes and stuffs them with leaves and straw to make dummies. The heads, she stuffs her red checkered scarf with straw. She then lines up the girls single file across from the dummies.

With a six-inch knife in hand, Loung stands at attention. Panting like an animal, with her legs shaking and her hand gripping the knife, Loung attacks at Met Srei's cue, charging at her dummy. Though she is focused on its head, Loung is only tall enough to thrust her knife into its stomach.

She stabs it over and over again.

Now she no longer has to pretend to be an orphan.

EXT. MUDDY FIELDS - DAY

Wide of the fields. Mounds of earth. It appears empty. Suddenly muddy girls rise up from their hiding places and run forward. Each holding a pointed stick in their hands. (possibly a few sticks to lay like traps)

Loung runs through the middy fields. She is covered in mud. She is fast. Angry. She pushes another little girl to the ground. She runs drops to her belly and crawls as if possessed.

EXT. CHILD SOLDIER TRAINING CAMP - NIGHT

JANUARY 1979

Hugging her rifle to her chest, Met Srei paces back and
forth.

                    MET SREI
          They will kill you if they catch
          you. You must protect yourself in
          anyway you can. Long live the
          glorious Cambodian revolution! Long
          live the great people of
          Kampuchea.

Fists in the air. Loung with ferocity. She seems older.
Something in her face has changed.

                    ALL
          Cheyo! Cheyo! Cheyo!

INT. CHILD SOLDIER TRAINING CAMP - NIGHT

That night none of the girls can sleep as they listen to
explosions of mortars and rockets in the distance. After a
few hours of shelling, all is quiet again.

Then without warning, a mortar explodes near their base,
blazing the sky white like lightning. Loung screams and
covers her ears with her hands just as another mortar
whistles and hits the camp. Trees burst into flame. Screaming
and wailing, the girls try to escape before fire consumes
them. The girls run and crawl away, their faces black from
smoke and their eyes white with terror. Many are dripping
blood from their arms and legs where shrapnel sliced through
their skin.

Loung heads away as the fire spreads everywhere.

                    GIRL'S VOICE
          Don't leave me! I'm hit! Help me!

Loung looks to see a girl lying in a pool of blood. Propping
herself up on her elbow, she begs for help. She is shaking
and shivering. The other girls do not stop. Seeing Loung
looking at her, she holds out a bloody hand to her. Fire
spreads through the camp quickly, debris falling everywhere.
Loung is much smaller than the girl. Loung screams and covers
her ears as another mortar explodes nearby. Panicked, she
turns her back on the girl and runs away.

The girl continues to scream long anguished cries as flames
engulf the camp.

All the girls head off in different directions in a desperate
bid to escape the camp. In the dark, the straw walls and
roofs combust into yellow and orange flames, illuminating the
red faces of girls running away.

EXT. ROAD - NIGHT

On the road, Loung finds herself crowded among hundreds of people walking amid deserted towns and villages. Automatically, her body takes control of her feet and veers her in the direction of her Chou's camp.

EXT. CHILDREN'S WORK CAMP - NIGHT

The camp is dark and empty when Loung get there.

                    LOUNG
              (desperate)
          Chou! Chou!

Loung circles around the compound, but Chou is not there. The camp has been evacuated. Penned animals panic as fire surrounds them.

EXT. ROAD - NIGHT

Loung runs back out into the traffic, not knowing what to do next. All around her the people move like a herd of cows. Not knowing what to do. She is afraid.

She feels a hand grab her shoulder. It's Kim. He's alive! Chou is with him, holding on tight to his hand. Loung's never been so happy!

                    KIM
          Come, we have to leave quickly.

Kim grabs Loung's hand and they head back onto the road and into the traffic.

Kim is once again in charge of the family. As other people carry their pots, pans, clothes, food, and other belongings on their backs or in their wagons, Kim carries a backpack with a few clothes in it, while Chou and Loung hold his hands and walk with only the clothes they are wearing.

EXT. ROAD - NIGHT TO SUNRISE

They walk with the sea of people, following their route. Loung leans on Kim. Soon the sun rises. In crimson red, golden yellow, and fiery orange, it lights up the world around them. In the field, tall elephant grass glistens with morning dew while gray smoke floats in to the sky from distant villages. The small red gravel roads are swarmed body to body with people in their black shirts and pants.

The traffic does not stop and continues to move, everybody dragging their feet slower and slower. Those who cannot move any farther sit at the side of the road, some curl up in a fetal position and sleep. The snakelike traffic pushes on with the strong able-bodied men forming the head, and the old, young, weak, and hungry trailing behind as the tail.

EXT. BOMBED HOUSE - MORNING

As the sun climbs higher in the sky. Kim spots a deserted bombed house. Chou and Loung follow Kim's lead.

EXT. BOMBED HOUSE- DAY

Alone in the bombed house, all is quiet except for the muffled grunts of pigs and cackles of chicken. The villagers evacuated in such a hurry that they left clothes, sandals, and scarves strewn everywhere on the ground. In the communal kitchen, smoke still rises from the ashes. Chou enters a hut and comes out with a few metal pots, aluminum bowls, and the remaining few small bags of rice and salt. Loung grabs three scarves, (or pieces like a jacket for Kim or a scarf for her?). Loung makes a big bundle with a scarf to balance on her head. Chou does the same.

Loung watches as Kim catch two chickens and locks their wings behind their backs. He kills them and hangs them to carry. (could be just one and may carry live)

OMITTED

EXT. ROAD - DAY

Bundles in hand, they walk back out to join the mob of people. Not knowing where they are going, they follow the traffic. Kim notices something on the road. He points it out to the girls. An anti tank mine. Half buried on the road. Loung looks at it as she carefully walks around it.

Later - they pass a land mine that has exploded. Nothing but **284** a hole in the ground and the remains of the blood from the victim who was dragged away. Now she is constantly looking down at the road. Terrified.

There is gunfire in the distance.

HOURS LATER

Loung stops and stares straight ahead.

Her heart pounds so loudly. Before them walk three men dressed in green clothes. Their legs move in long, casual strides and their rifles swing on their back. "Youns," the traffic hums and whispers. Loung is surprised as she was told they are like monsters. In fact they are the same size as Khmer men and are similarly built. They do not look like the devils Met Srei said they were.

The Vietnamese walk toward them and raise their hands in greeting. Loung searches the ground for weapons - a staff, sharp rocks, anything she can use to fight them. All eyes focus on them as they come nearer. People gasp when, in the next moment, one Vietnamese smiles.

> VIETNAMESE SOLDIER
> (in broken Khemer)
> Chum reap sour. (hello) There is a
> rest area ahead in Pursat City.

At last, they have a destination. Loung, Kim and Chou carefully walk past the soldier. Still not feeling completely safe around him. They walk on.

EXT. INTERNALLY DISPLACED AREA - LATE DAY

Loung sees the area. It looms like a small village before them, flickering and swaying in the haze like a mirage.

Many people are very thin. Those who were not in labor or soldier camps are near dead.

Next to the tents, women prepare food (caught snake, frogss or chicken) , blowing and stoking the fires, coughing as the smoke finds their faces.

The Vietnamese are all around, weaving through the labyrinth and patrolling the area with rifles on their shoulders and grenades attached to their belts.

Kim pulls at Loung's arm and gestures for her to hurry as she begins to fall behind. They pass through the crowd, searching for an empty spot to make their home.

Kim, Loung, and Chou settle under a tree at the edge of the area with a few other ORPHANS.

EXT. INTERNALLY DISPLACED AREA - LATE DAY

Loung Kim and Chou pluck the chickens.

EXT. INTERNALLY DISPLACED AREA - DUSK

Finally Chou announces they are done. Kim breaks off a leg, scoops up a bowl of rice, and hands it to Loung. With their plates in front of them, they eat in silence.

They notice a couple Orphans staring. Chou whispers to Kim and he invites them to share what little chicken they have.

EXT. INTERNALLY DISPLACED AREA - DAY

A day in the area - add details. Chou and Loung preparing a snake (with a knife they found at the abandoned house). Kim prepares a fire.

Survival. Some cooking frogs or spiders.

Some people dying, having been starved too long.

Later-

Kim brings over a small water bucket. Kim, Chou and Loung help each other clean up. Chou wipes mud off Loung's face. She then runs her fingers through her hair to "brush" it.

Chou then walks up to Kim and pulls stray threads from his shirt.

EXT. INTERNALLY DISPLACED AREA - NIGHT

Chou spreads out their scarfs and lies down. With her in the middle, Kim and Loung huddle closely on either side of her. Kim hooks a bundle through his arms while Loung does the same to her bundle. They pull (Kims new jacket?) over themselves.

All around them people are sleeping, eating, or sitting quietly together. Many who have little strength left are assisting the sick. Loung looks over to the side and watches a family sitting together, eating their meal. It is a family of five, parents with three boys, from perhaps five to ten years old. The father scoops rice and hands it over to his youngest child first, then he does the same for the others. The mother reaches over and wipes the child's nose with her fingers, then quickly wipes her hand on her skirt. Loung looks at the fathers kind eyes. She sees how much he loves his family. She misses Pa.

Loung turns away.

Gunfire can be heard in the distance.

INT. INTERNALLY DISPLACED AREA - DAY

Loung and Chou wash and hang their laundry.

MEMORY

INT. PHNOM PENH APARTMENT - MORNING

Flashes - New Year's morning, Keav, with big pink, yellow, blue, and green prickly plastic rollers in her hair held in by a hundred small black bobby pins sticking up everywhere like porcupine quills, as she combs Loung's hair and ties it in ponytails. Next to her on the bed, Chou works on getting Geak dressed. After Keav finishes with Loung's hair, she puts red rouge on Geak's lips and cheeks.

On their bed, they bounce with glee as their mattress squeaks. Colors and pretty clothes and laughter.

MEMORY ENDS

An ax chops wood—

EXT. WOODS - EARLY MORNING

Loung, Kim and Chou gather firewood. Loung steps on something that looks like a brown twig but it slithers away giving her a small fright.

Loung rubs her tired eyes, yawns, and adjusts the ropes she brought to tie the firewood, slinging them over her shoulders. Chou walks ahead with the ax in her arms.

EXT. INTERNALLY DISPLACED AREA - DAWN

FEBRUARY 1979

The sounds of morning. The mass of small makeshift settlements for displaced families are all silent. Men in green patrol the area.

EXT. INTERNALLY DISPLACED AREA - DAWN

Suddenly Loung awakens to the sound of a loud explosion. She bolts upright, her ears ringing from the blast. She hears a shrilling whine before another rocket ruptures nearby. The children scream at the top of their lungs, clambering around the campsite. Loung, Chou, Kim and the Orphans move.

EXT. INTERNALLY DISPLACED AREA - CONTINUOUS - DAWN

The earth shakes violently as crackling yellow, orange, and red flames devour a nearby hut. Gray smoke floats to the sky and white ashes fall on them like powder. (if no hut then embers from a blast. To be discussed)

Loung watches as all around her people cry and scream for help as more rockets rain on the village. Fire engulfs the camp and villagers rush to evacuate.

EXT. INTERNALLY DISPLACED AREA - DAWN

Loung sees the men in green fighting the KR soldiers. Both sides seem equally frightening to her.

Loung gets separated. She looks around everyone looks the same. She can't find Kim and Chou. She feels panicked.

Finally, she finds them. With their legs shaking in fear, they follow Kim ducking and keeping low.

EXT. RIVER - MORNING

They come to the river and, holding hands, wade into it. The river splashes in waves as hundreds of people jump in it at once trying to get to the other side. With small bundles on their heads or draped on their shoulders and small children hanging on their backs, the villagers wade across the chest-deep stream, desperately reaching for safety. Loung Kim and Chou tuck in to the side of the river bank to avoid the battle that rages around them. RE IMAGE AJP.

She sees a young KR fighting the Vietnamese. It's Smiling Boy.

A blast almost knocks the air out from Loung's lungs. She reaches for the Orphan boy's arm, then jerks her hand back as her palm touches something wet and sticky on her.

Her stomach churns. Loung turns to see him lying facedown on the ground, quiet and motionless. His little brother below him covered in blood. The top of his skull is caved in. A pool of blood slowly seeps into the dirt around her head. Blood and pieces of brain are on Loung's hand.

EXT. RIVER - MORNING

The battle rages on. Loung, Chou and Kim are under fire and forced to run.

EXT. FOREST - MORNING

People are scattered everywhere, soaking wet screaming and crying as they run in every direction, bumping and pushing each other. Kim and Chou hold hands and run ahead of Loung, yelling for her to keep up. They don't know where to run to, they just run.

EXT. FOREST - MORNING

Running as fast as she can, Loung jumps over dead bodies. She hears their bullets whiz past her. She runs for her life. In front of her, a man falls from a bullet. His body stops mid stride, his chest jerking forward before he falls to the ground. Many people get hit and drop one by one to the ground all around her. Some lie still while others crawl on their elbows trying to reach safety.

Loung sees a man thrown into the air as the ground explodes beneath him. Land mines. She keeps running. A woman with child stands screaming. Another woman running knocks into her and the ground beneath them explodes. Loung runs staring at the ground. What can she do? Bullets from behind, land mines underneath. She holds her breath and moves forward. (Possibly moves forward slowly because of mines. Could discuss slow motion as world blows up around her and her heart beats)

Minutes later-

After she catches up with Chou and Kim, they see an old remnant of a tree stump. It sticks out of the ground three feet tall by four feet wide. They crouch behind it.

EXT. TREE STUMP - DAY

Chou covers her ears with her hands and squeezes her eyes
shut. Kim is white, leaning against the tree for support.
They stay there for what seems like hours until all is quiet
again.

Later-

When they believe it is safe, they come out from behind the
tree stump.

Loung watches Chou and Kim trudge ahead, their eyes focusing
on the ground.

There are smoldering remains of bonfires giving off the
stench of burnt human flesh all through the village. Trails
and puddles of blood stain the area. Her eyes are on the
ground wherever she goes, steering clear of anything that
looks like a grenade or land mine. They try to step into the
footprints of others.

EXT. BORDER CAMP - DAY

A month or so later. They have moved with others up to a more
mountainous region where it is safe. Chou and Loung at the
river. Life is returning. We can see that aid relief is
beginning to trickle in.

EXT. BORDER CAMP - DAY

Kim arrives at the site all flushed and out of breath.

As he explains this, Loung hears every other word

                    KIM
            (out of breath)
        A Khmer Rouge soldier. They caught
        him. (Pointing) They are taking him
        up there.

Kim sits to catch his breath.

Loung pulls Chou with her. She wants to see. Chou resists.
Loung heads off on her own.

EXT. BORDER CAMP - DAY

Loung makes her way towards the sound until she closes in on
a mob of people.

Their bodies block her view of the prisoner. She tries to
shift her body to find an open space but she cannot.
Frustrated, she wedges her small body between theirs and
pushes her way through. She is in the middle of the crowd,
surrounded by people. She cannot see anything. She looks up
to the faces of the adults who are all looking in the same
direction. Some are staring at him overwhelmed with emotion,
unable to speak. Some are full of rage.

Finally, she sees a clearing between people's legs. She tries
to push her way through, but they are so engrossed in what's
going on that they do not move. Determined, she gets on her
hands and knees, and crawls through the brown forest of legs
up to the front.

There he is. Loung stands and finds herself almost face-to-
face with him, separated by only ten feet. Automatically, she
raises her scarf to cover her head and face. Her heart beats
wildly. Fear seeps into her body. She peeks over her scarf.
He is looking at her.

She takes a step back, leaning into the crowd for protection.
The crowd vibrates with anticipation and energy, closing in
around the prisoner. Loung's hands close into fists.

The mans face reveals nothing. His lips do not beg for mercy.
He sits propped up on a high back chair on a gravel hill that
serves as a stage. He is dark and wears the black clothes of
the Khmer Rouge. A rough hemp rope that binds his feet
together. More rope straps him to the back of the chair, it
coils around him from the chest down to the stomach.

> CROWD
> Murderer!

Loung stares at him full of hatred.

Loung watches as sweat streams down his adams apple. He bends
his head, looks down at his feet again, knowing there is no
way out.

Many people are wailing and accusing the man of killing their
loved ones. Begging him to answer for his crimes.

A WOMAN, crying loudly, pushes her way to the front of the
crowd. She is young, in her mid twenties. Like Loung, she
wears the Khmer Rouge clothes. Though tears fall from her
eyes, her face is angry.

> WOMAN
> (shaking with emotion)
> I know this soldier. He killed my
> husband and my sons. I know this
> man.

Tears in her eyes. In her hand she holds a weapon, its wooden
handle worn and splintered. Loung no longer listening. She is
fixated on the prisoner. He looks up briefly when the women
comes forth, but now he is back in position, head down, eyes
to the ground.

Loung watches as the woman walks up to him, her weapon in
hand. She stands in front of him, staring at the top of his
head. Loung wants to shield her eyes from what's about to
happen, but she can't. The woman's hands shake as she raises
the weapon high above her head.

(FLASH OF PA BEING HIT.)

The woman raises her weapon again.

The crowd is silenced.

An OLDER WOMAN reaches for her to stop her. She pushes her
away. A man steps forward angry and is held back by another.
There is pain and chaos. Screaming and tears.

Blood splatters the woman's clothes, and face. She screams
and swings the weapon up above her head again. (Flash of
Loung with a weapon. A surreal moment) Blood droplets land on
Loung's pants and face as she stands watching. Loung watches
as the prisoners leg jerks but is held down by the rope. The
Khmer Rouge body convulses and trembles, as if electricity is
traveling to the legs, arms, and fingers.

The Older Woman grabs her and holds her. She regains her
composure. The Older Woman speaks with passion about how the
Cambodian people will not be destroyed by this. That she will
not become hateful like the KR.

Then the Woman drops the weapon and they begin to walk away.
When they turn around, Loung sees that she looks like death
herself. Her hair trickles blood and sweat, their clothes
drip, her face red and rigid. (flash cuts between Loung and
the Woman)

The Woman is quiet as the crowd parts for her to pass
through.

Moments later- One by one, people return to their homes,
leaving Loung standing there alone, staring at the KR
soldier. He looks back at her.

Loung's fists open. She no longer wants to fight.

(THIS IS ONE OF THE MOST IMPORTANT CINEMATIC MOMENTS AND WILL
BE HELD ON FOR A LOT OF SCREEN TIME TO MAKE THE POINT AND BE
AN IMAGE BURNED INTO THE MIND. THE DAUGHTER OF CAMBODIA AND
THE BEATEN KR SOLDIER. BLOOD AND SILENCE.)

Finally, Loung cries. She lets it all come out of her. All
the loss. All the pain.

BORDER CAMP - EARLY MORNING

1979

Sun rises over the large camp.

Loung watches a young man who was a victim of a land-mine
months ago. Now he helps to build a small hut. She is in awe
of his strength and agility with his loss of limbs.

She looks around the camp. Some people have already changed
into colorful clothes. More plastic tents.

EXT. BORDER CAMP- EARLY MORNING

Light rain falls on Loung's small frame. Still in her old
black pants, she wears a new colorful shirt. Her hair is now
longer.

She balls up a handful of rice and rolls it into a banana
leaf. She walks over to a woman sleeping alone under another
tree. A small child lay nearby. She lays it down in front of
her as a silent gift.

EXT. BORDER CAMP - MORNING

Like in the opening she walks and sees her reflection. This
time in the pond. She walks on towards a tree. She climbs up
a tree. She looks across the camp. She looks down at her
feet. So much has changed since her days in Phnom Penh.

Loung hears Kim and looks up. She sees Kim walking towards
her with two men. Afraid, she jumps down and takes a step
back.

She can't see clearly. Chou is also staring at the men. As
they comes closer they realize it is Meng and Khouy!

Chou runs to them and jumps into Khouy's arms. Loung finds
herself feeling shy, and stands stiff and awkward. Meng
kneels before her. He smiles and musses her hair just like
he used to. Her heart soars quickly at the touch of his
hand. He is real - not a figment of her imagination!

Her brothers are alive. The five remaining members of the family embrace each other. They have survived.

We hold on Loung's face. She smiles.

THE END

A shot of the real Loung, Chou, Kim, Meng and Khouy walking together in Cambodia. They are in a beautiful temple. We pan to the faces in stone. The faces that look like Pa-

IN MEMORY OF THE TWO MILLION PEOPLE WHO PERISHED UNDER THE KHMER ROUGE

AND FOR THOSE WHO SURVIVED

Close on Loung and Chou smiling at each other.

END CREDITS

99890846R00052